DI

P9-CKN-996

3 1193 00261 6502

tion

VERY SHORT INTRODUCTIONS are for anyone wanting a stimulating and accessible way in to a new subject. They are written by experts, and have been published in more than 25 languages worldwide.

The series began in 1995, and now represents a wide variety of topics in history, philosophy, religion, science, and the humanities. The VSI Library now contains over 200 volumes—a Very Short Introduction to everything from ancient Egypt and Indian philosophy to conceptual art and cosmology—and will continue to grow to a library of around 300 titles.

Very Short Introductions available now:

For more information visit our web site
www.oup.co.uk/general/vsi/

Scott H. Hendrix

MARTIN LUTHER

A Very Short Introduction

OXFORD
UNIVERSITY PRESS

OXFORD

UNIVERSITY PRESS

Great Clarendon Street, Oxford OX2 6DP

Oxford University Press is a department of the University of Oxford.
It furthers the University's objective of excellence in research, scholarship,
and education by publishing worldwide in

Oxford New York

Auckland Cape Town Dar es Salaam Hong Kong Karachi
Kuala Lumpur Madrid Melbourne Mexico City Nairobi
New Delhi Shanghai Taipei Toronto

With offices in

Argentina Austria Brazil Chile Czech Republic France Greece
Guatemala Hungary Italy Japan Poland Portugal Singapore
South Korea Switzerland Thailand Turkey Ukraine Vietnam

Oxford is a registered trade mark of Oxford University Press
in the UK and in certain other countries

Published in the United States
by Oxford University Press Inc., New York

© Scott H. Hendrix 2010

The moral rights of the author have been asserted
Database right Oxford University Press (maker)

First published 2010

All rights reserved. No part of this publication may be reproduced,
stored in a retrieval system, or transmitted, in any form or by any means,
without the prior permission in writing of Oxford University Press,
or as expressly permitted by law, or under terms agreed with the appropriate
reprographics rights organization. Enquiries concerning reproduction
outside the scope of the above should be sent to the Rights Department,
Oxford University Press, at the address above

You must not circulate this book in any other binding or cover
and you must impose the same condition on any acquirer

British Library Cataloguing in Publication Data

Data available

Library of Congress Cataloging in Publication Data

Data available

Typeset by SPI Publisher Services, Pondicherry, India
Printed in Great Britain by
Ashford Colour Press Ltd, Gosport, Hampshire

ISBN: 978–0–19–957433–9

10 9 8 7 6 5 4 3 2 1

In Memoriam
Helmar Junghans
(1931–2010)

Martin Luther, by Lucas Cranach, 1533

Contents

Foreword

In 2010, Martin Luther arrived on Twitter, a medium ideal for a very short introduction since only 140 characters were allowed. This book has a few more words, but it is intended nonetheless to be a brief introduction to the life and work of a man who himself frequently used more words than necessary. Despite his verbosity, Martin Luther was an interesting and controversial writer whose words made history – to the enthusiasm of some and to the dismay of others. Those words influenced not only the way German is still spoken and written but also the dynamics of religion and culture in the modern world. Luther stressed the power of words in general and, as befitted a theologian, the efficaciousness of divine words in particular, but this book is mainly about his own words and the impact they had on his 16th-century European world. As such, it is neither a biography nor a theology of Luther but a series of snapshots that attempt to capture his life and relationships, his agenda and his work, his perceptions and prejudices, the faith and the feelings of a human being who was rarely at a loss for words and, because of that, disclosed more of himself than most people would dare.

The book contains no footnotes or endnotes, but the sources for quotations and paraphrases of what Luther wrote are readily located in vernacular editions of his writings that are mentioned in the text. Some translations of what Luther wrote are, however, my own. I am happy to provide documentation if you contact me through the publisher or at scott.hendrix@ptsem.edu. For the sake of space and clarity, I have simplified the history at a few points. For example, Luther was never a cloistered monk but a 'brother' or friar who lived in Augustinian houses in Erfurt and Wittenberg that were not cloisters in the strictest sense. Nevertheless, Luther referred to himself as a monk, wrote a critique of 'monastic vows', and did not make a sharp distinction between cloistered monks and friars like Augustinians, Franciscans, and Dominicans. It would have been artificial and unnecessary to avoid the words 'cloister', 'monk', and 'monastery' throughout the book.

I am indebted to all the people – teachers, colleagues, and students – from whom I have learned about the Reformation and especially to those who over the years have challenged me to think differently about it. For this book, I am grateful to the readers of my manuscript for their suggestions and especially to Emma Marchant of Oxford University Press for her steady encouragement and astute advice. I am also pleased to acknowledge and publicly thank Sandra Kimball, the indexer of this book and of my three previous books. Her knowledge of the 16th century combined with her skill and precision have made these books more useful to readers than they otherwise would have been.

This book is dedicated to the memory of Helmar Junghans, longtime editor of the *Lutherjahrbuch* and professor of church history at Leipzig. His incomparable knowledge of Luther was shared generously with me and others over many years filled with friendship and hospitality. He died during a bicycle tour just one week before this book was finished.

Scott H. Hendrix
Pentecost 2010

List of illustrations

Luther sites in Germany

Chapter 1
Luther and the Reformation

At four o'clock on Wednesday afternoon, 17 April 1521, a 37-year-old excommunicated monk and university professor, Martin Luther, stood before the dignitaries of the Holy Roman Empire gathered for their Diet, a costly, drawn-out assembly which addressed urgent financial and military matters and, in this case, heresy. One day earlier, Luther had reached the German city of Worms on the Rhine after a two-week journey that resembled a victory parade more than a solemn procession that could end with his death. Emperor Charles V, only 21 years old and two years in office, had summoned Luther to Worms for him to recant the books he had written, books now piled on the table before him in the bishop's palatial residence next to the cathedral. Although Luther held out hope for a fair hearing in Worms, the deck was stacked against him. The official in charge told Luther he was permitted to answer only two questions: Was he the author of the books that had been published in his name? If yes, did he stand by what he had written or did he wish to recant anything he had said?

To this point, the story of Martin Luther at Worms may be familiar, especially if his refusal to recant and the famous final words ('here I stand, I cannot do otherwise, God help me, amen') are considered to be his answer. For the last half century, scholars have suspected that the words 'here I stand, I cannot do otherwise', which inspired the title of a popular biography by Roland Bainton, were not spoken by Luther. Nonetheless, they made his reputation as the defiant and heroic initiator of the Protestant Reformation, a reputation bolstered over the years by writers, film-makers, and artists who depicted this scene and his nailing of the Ninety-Five Theses in 1517 as the deeds of a rebel against authority and defender of individual freedom. Those depictions are misleading. If the Theses were in fact posted, Luther was only giving notice of an academic debate; and at Worms, he requested a day's respite to draft his response to the questions about his books. The answer he read to the Diet on 18 April 1521 turned out to be milder and more complex than a tirade against authority. Some of his writings, he acknowledged, contained harsher criticism of his opponents than befitted a monk, but, he continued, the laws of the pope and church teachings had so tortured the consciences of laity that, if he recanted his writings, he would 'reinforce tyranny and fling open not just the windows but also the doors to a great ungodliness'. Luther was also mindful of his own conscience, to which he appealed in the oft-quoted conclusion that he called a simple answer with no strings attached: 'Unless I am convinced by the testimony of the scriptures or indisputable argument, I am bound by the scriptures I have quoted and my conscience is captive to the word of God.'

Martin Luther did not found a Western tradition of religious liberty, nor did he set out to defy pope and emperor to defend modern notions of democracy. In their breadth known to us, such ideas were beyond him, although Luther's struggle for Christian freedom, as he called it in 1520, did anticipate later struggles for religious freedom. Nor did he storm the barricades by design. The Reformation, he contended, was not a premeditated campaign but a reaction to his writings. Once Luther questioned in public the theology he had learned and the piety that surrounded him, the religious authorities that profited from practices like indulgences felt threatened. At Rome, the pope's advisors opened

> In his book, Bainton quoted the last sentence of Luther's speech as it was recorded in the minutes of the Diet, where Luther says only 'God help me, amen'. The first part of the sentence, 'here I stand…', appeared only in the sympathetic Latin account of Luther's hearing that was printed first in Wittenberg and can be read in volume seven of the Weimar edition. Bainton speculated as follows about the first part of the sentence: 'The words, though not recorded on the spot, may nevertheless be genuine, because the listeners at the moment may have been too moved to write.'
>
> (*Here I Stand*, p. 185)

an investigation that led to his excommunication after Luther found no persuasive historical or biblical evidence for their claims of papal supremacy. There was no proof, he said, that the apostle Peter, whom the popes claimed to succeed, was ever present in Rome, and the words of Jesus about building the church on a rock associated with Peter's name had nothing to do with popes or their authority. His opponents, Luther said, could not refute his critique of indulgences so they attacked his audacity to place limits on papal power. His proposals, however, to change the practice of Christianity so that it conformed more closely to scripture brought him support from scholars and the public alike. By the time he arrived at Worms in 1521, he was on his way to becoming the most popular author in Germany and, unlike his predecessors, the successful leader of a religious reform movement that expanded worldwide and lasted into the 21st century.

After Luther and most of the delegates had departed Worms, Emperor Charles V issued an edict that outlawed Luther and his supporters. Having anticipated the edict, Luther's supportive prince, Elector Frederick the Wise of Saxony, ordered that Luther's party be intercepted on its way home and Luther installed at a secret location that turned out to be the Wartburg fortress near Eisenach – over 100 miles south-west of Wittenberg, the small town where Luther lived and taught. Frederick appreciated the publicity Luther had brought to his fledgling university, but now the elector was faced with the dilemma of what to do with his excommunicated and outlawed professor. Once the emperor's edict was published, the prince and his Saxon lands became vulnerable, and Frederick decided to keep Luther out of circulation. While Luther was away, his colleagues in Wittenberg, led by Andrew Karlstadt, did not wait to take action. They capitalized on local feeling to make the first visible changes in worship and religious life that turned ideas into action. The changes, however, stirred up unrest and alarmed the Wittenberg city council, which urged Luther to return. Against the wishes of Elector Frederick, Luther left the Wartburg in March of 1522 and resumed leadership of 'his flock' in Wittenberg. Karlstadt was soon pushed aside, and Luther took over the reformation that altered European culture and made him a public figure to be remembered.

For years, visitors to Luther's quarters in the Wartburg fortress were shown a spot where an inkwell, thrown by Luther at the devil, had hit the wall. The first story involving an inkwell dates to the end of the 16th century, when a former Wittenberg student claimed to have heard that the devil, dressed as a monk, threw an inkwell at the reformer. The first book to refer to an inkspot on the wall appeared in 1650, and thereafter the traditional story featured Luther throwing an inkwell at the devil. Gradually, an inkspot appeared on the walls of other buildings where Luther had lived and the story became a widely enjoyed legend. Equally spurious are reports that Luther, while at the Wartburg, was visited by the devil in the forms of a fly buzzing around his head and a large black dog in his bed.

As a political or philosophical thinker, Martin Luther was not the first to be modern, but he was the last medieval reformer, because his reforms succeeded where others had failed to alter the landscape of Europe. Without the Reformation, which outgrew him and his early followers, Luther would have remained another unfortunate – probably executed – critic of the medieval Roman Church in a line of sincere reformers with at best a modest legacy. In Worms, the monument that commemorates him also memorializes four excommunicated reformers who preceded him, one each from Bohemia, Italy, France, and England. Luther stands tall at the centre since he survived both excommunication and the threat of execution to become a hero in the eyes of 19th-century Protestants who erected the memorial. A word about these predecessors will make clear why Martin Luther's escape from execution was only one reason that he was the most influential of them all. No other medieval reformer initiated a religious movement that attained the geographical scope and political support enjoyed by the 16th-century Protestant Reformation.

The earliest of Luther's forerunners to occupy a corner of the monument was Peter Waldo, a prosperous 12th-century merchant from the French city of Lyons. Like Francis of Assisi, Waldo acted on a common medieval impulse and surrendered his wealth and property to walk in the footsteps of Jesus and the earliest apostles. Unlike Francis, however, Waldo and his lay followers never received papal permission to preach or to form a new order. Hence they flouted church authority and preached without approval, using partial translations of the Bible in dialect and quickly gaining adherents in both southern France and Italy. After criticizing the pomp of the church and practices like praying for the dead and indulgences, these Waldensians, or Poor Men of Lyons as they were called in France, were finally declared heretics and excommunicated in 1184. Despite this stigma, the Waldensians survived the Inquisition by emigrating to other parts of Europe, hiding in small units tucked away in the Alps, and by organizing a modest church. Most Waldensians later affiliated with the Calvinist wing of the Protestant Reformation, but that did not immunize them against banishment and persecution. After an unprovoked slaughter of Italian Waldensians in 1655, the poet John Milton honoured their ideals and suffering in his 18th sonnet 'On the Late Massacre in Piedmont'.

The second of Luther's predecessors to occupy a corner of the monument was the Oxford don John Wyclif (d. 1384). Long regarded as the first translator of the Bible into English, Wyclif was more of a philosopher than a biblical scholar or religious activist. Nonetheless, his name was linked to the peasants' revolt of 1381 and to clandestine Lollard groups that circulated unauthorized translations of scripture that did not come from his pen. Wyclif questioned the church's right to exercise civil dominion over property and argued that an immoral priest forfeited the right to exercise his office and was possibly excluded from the church in its truest sense – the community of righteous believers whom God had predestined to salvation. For all these reasons and more, Wyclif was accused of heresy and his beliefs were condemned by the pope, the University of Oxford, and by a general church council. In seclusion at Lutterworth during the last two years of his life, Wyclif may have suffered a stroke before he died in 1384. He was buried in the churchyard, but in 1428, by order of Pope Martin V, his bones were exhumed, burned, and deposited in the River Swift.

Many of Wyclif's writings survived his death, owing especially to the popularity of his ideas among Czech scholars. Some of them had studied at Oxford, copied his works, and returned with them to Prague, where they were read by John Hus, the third pre-Reformation figure on the Worms monument. Hus was both a scholar and a popular spokesman for reformist ideas. In 1402, he was chosen rector of the university and appointed the main preacher at Bethlehem chapel, a privately endowed church founded in 1391 to serve the university and the people of Prague.

From its pulpit, Hus attacked indulgences, simony (buying ecclesiastical office), and papal immorality. Like Wyclif, he argued that the true church was the community of predestined believers, and his own treatise on the subject incorporated passages from Wyclif's book. Bitterly opposed by the German professors who had condemned the 45 propositions of Wyclif, Hus eventually lost the backing of his archbishop and was excommunicated by the pope. In 1414, he was summoned to a general council of the church at Constance in southern Germany. King Sigismund failed to protect him as promised, and Hus was imprisoned for a year, accused of holding the heretical opinions of Wyclif that were condemned by the council, put on trial after a fashion, and found guilty. His protestations fell on deaf ears. After being mocked and humiliated as a heretic, Hus was burned at the stake on 6 July 1415, and his ashes strewn over the Rhine.

Hus left behind sympathetic colleagues and a *bona fide* reform movement in his homeland of Bohemia. Incensed at his execution and inflamed by nationalistic feeling, his Czech followers rose up against their king and the Roman Church. For their standard they chose the chalice, a symbol of their demand to receive at Mass the wine that had been withheld from them and reserved for the priests. Because they celebrated Mass by giving both elements, bread and wine, to all communicants, the moderate Hussites were called Utraquists (from the Latin term for 'both'). After a series of battles failed to suppress the Hussite revolt, the demands of the Utraquists were granted by the Council of Basel (1431), and they survived as the Bohemian Brethren alongside a minority of Catholics loyal to Rome until the Thirty Years War (1618–48). That conflict started after two Catholic officials, with their secretary, were hurled from the windows of Prague Castle by disgruntled Protestants who accused the three men of undermining their religious freedom. Although the three men landed in a pile of manure and survived, the incident led to a Protestant defeat and the end of the Hussite reformation.

The last forerunner of Luther depicted on the Worms monument was Girolamo Savonarola (1452–98), a Dominican friar excommunicated by Pope Alexander VI and then executed when his efforts to transform Florence into a Christian republic backfired. After French forces had banished the Medici family and left him as the *de facto* ruler of Florence, Savonarola and his supporters made every effort to suppress vice and frivolity in the city. Gambling and expensive dress were restrained by sumptuary laws, and in 1497 women flocked to the public square to toss their cosmetics, mirrors, fancy dresses, and costly ornaments onto a huge 'bonfire of the vanities'. Savonarola had justified these measures in fervent sermons based on private visions that prophesied a new age of the spirit after the world was cleansed through terrible tribulations. When Savonarola refused to obey a summons to appear in Rome, the pope threatened to prohibit the entire city from receiving the sacraments. Lacking French support, the people turned against Savonarola. A mob broke into the monastery of San Marco, seized the prophet and two associates, and turned them over to civic officials. They were interrogated and tortured, and on 23 May 1498, all three were hanged in the middle of the city and their corpses burned.

The designers of the monument in Worms had good reasons to portray the Waldensians, Wyclif, Hus, and Savonarola as forerunners of Luther. They had many things in common with the German reformer. The Bible was the source of their proposals to reform Christian life, and they supported partial translations into the vernacular so that ordinary people could read scripture for themselves. The teaching of Jesus and the portrayal of early Christians in the New Testament were ideals their followers were encouraged to achieve. Preaching was a powerful tool for the dissemination of their ideas, and they continued to preach even after they were discouraged or excommunicated. They criticized clerical conduct and challenged papal authority. Sufficient political toleration and support were available for their reforms to survive for a spell in France, Italy, England, and Bohemia. Reform was an ancient ideal in Christianity, and most attempts to implement changes throughout its history, even monastic renewal, had one or more of these features.

What made Luther different from the other reformers who share with him the monument in Worms? With respect to John Hus, the forerunner about whom he knew the most, Luther himself answered the question more than once. During a debate at Leipzig in 1519, the Catholic theologian John Eck charged that Luther held three of Hus's heretical opinions. In reply, Luther denounced the Hussites as Bohemian schismatics, but he also declared that some of Hus's statements condemned at Constance were quite evangelical and Christian. Later that year, two Utraquists in Prague sent Luther a copy of Hus's book on the church. He must have read it quickly, for in early 1520 Luther described its impact:

> Until now I have held and espoused all the teachings of John Hus
> without knowing it.... In short we are all Hussites without realizing
> it.... I am dumbfounded when I see such terrible judgments of God
> upon us. The most obvious evangelical truth, which was publicly
> burned more than one hundred years ago, is condemned and no
> one is allowed to confess it.

These words, which admit of little or no distinction between the reformers, seemed to fulfil a popular prophecy attributed 11 years later by Luther to the imprisoned Hus: 'Now they will roast this goose (for Hus means goose), but one hundred years hence they will hear the song of a swan which they shall have to tolerate.' No record exists of Hus having made this prophecy, but its fulfilment in Luther was endorsed by his followers in writing and in pictures that placed a swan next to the German reformer.

Luther did not always identify himself with Hus. In 1520, he claimed that Hus's criticism of the papacy did not go far enough and that he, Luther, had done five times as much. In his *Table Talk*, edited versions of Luther's mealtime conversations, Hus was criticized for clinging to the 'superstition of the private mass' and for caring more about upright behaviour than correct teaching:

> Doctrine and conduct must be distinguished. Conduct is bad among us as it is among the papists, but we don't fight about conduct or condemn the papists on that account. Wyclif and Hus did not know this and attacked the papacy for its behaviour…[Attacking doctrine] is my calling.

In all likelihood, Luther was referring to the writings of Wyclif and Hus against simony and clerical immorality, but the sharp distinction he drew between doctrine and conduct was exaggerated. Although Luther insisted that the chief doctrine of Christianity was not about morality but about faith, he also said that true faith was inseparable from active love and compassion. In a sermon preached after his return to Wittenberg in 1522, Luther scolded his listeners:

> You are willing to take all the good things God offers in the sacrament, but you are not willing to pour them out again in love.…Such a pity! You have heard many sermons about it and all my books are full of it and have this one purpose: to urge you to faith and love.

Luther came closer to explaining why he and not his forerunners initiated the Reformation when he said that Hus wrote against indulgences before the time was ripe. The monument at Worms suggests why it was ripe in 1517, when Luther's Ninety-Five Theses on the power of indulgences, a Latin text prepared for academic debate, unleashed a politically charged religious movement that could not be contained. At the front corners of the monument stand the most significant political leaders of the German Protestant movement: Landgrave Philip of Hesse and Elector Frederick the Wise of Saxony. Without the protection of Elector Frederick and his successors, Luther would not have survived the edict pronounced against him and his followers at Worms; and without the military and political clout of Philip of Hesse, an early advocate of the evangelical movement, Protestants might not have fended off attempts by Emperor Charles V to stop the Reformation. Allegorical figures of three German cities – Magdeburg, Speyer, and Augsburg – also grace the monument and stand for the crucial role played by free cities of the empire that adopted the Reformation and stood firmly behind it. At Augsburg in 1530, Lutherans presented to the emperor a defence of their faith that became known as the Augsburg Confession, but Charles V refused to accept it. In 1555, however, also at Augsburg, German Protestants who adhered to that confession were given legal status in the Holy Roman Empire, and Charles V gave up his campaign against them.

The rear corners of the monument support statues of Philip Melanchthon, a younger colleague of Luther, Greek scholar, and co-leader of the Lutheran movement, and of Johannes Reuchlin, a renowned Hebrew scholar and Melanchthon's mentor. Both men represent the influence of German Humanism on the Reformation. Hus and Wyclif were also scholars, but they did not benefit from the intense study of languages or the surge of printed material that followed the invention of movable type in the 1450s. Most reformers in the 16th century had Humanist training and could read the Bible in Hebrew and Greek. Thanks to scholars like Erasmus of Rotterdam, critical editions of scripture, of classical authors, and of early church theologians like Augustine became available to Luther.

The work of his colleagues and other reformers was also indispensable to the spread of the Reformation. Portrait medallions on the Worms monument picture four of those co-workers. John Bugenhagen, pastor and professor in Wittenberg, carried the evangelical movement to northern Germany and Denmark and, because he was from Pomerania and knew the Low German dialect of the north, was able to compose constitutions for the new Lutheran churches in those lands. Justus

Jonas, both a colleague and friend of Luther in Wittenberg, reformed other towns with his preaching and with his facility to translate Luther's Latin into German for a wider readership. Ulrich Zwingli, a Swiss Humanist who preached directly from the Greek New Testament, brought to Zürich and its environs a reformed movement that was distinct from German Lutheranism and later allied itself with John Calvin, the French-born reformer of Geneva, whose influence spread to many parts of Europe. Calvinism was more influential than Lutheranism on the Reformation in England that made it a Protestant country after 1559.

Not all reasons for the success of the 16th-century Reformation stem directly from Luther or Wittenberg, although it is impossible to say whether or not extensive reform would have occurred without him. It is not speculation, however, to say that Martin Luther would not appear in this series without the religious revolution that exceeded any reform he imagined and had far greater consequences for the modern world than the initiatives of his predecessors.

Chapter 2
Becoming a reformer

With 37 years behind him, Martin Luther was well into middle age by the time of his friendly kidnapping after the Diet of Worms. Although he did not realize it, along with his professorship – if he was allowed to keep it – Luther was starting a second career. The ten months spent at the Wartburg (May 1521 to March 1522) were filled with study, writing, and reflection that convinced Luther of a new calling. He was no longer a monk but a divinely led servant destined to recover for Germany a truer version of Christianity than medieval religion, which to him appeared corrupt and full of superstition. How did the son of a mining entrepreneur from a small town in Germany come to this radical view of himself?

Luther called his parents poor and himself the son of a peasant, but those words give a false impression of his childhood. His father Hans was the son of a farmer in the small village of Möhra not far from the town of Eisenach that was the home of Luther's mother, Margarete Lindemann. Her relatives were well-established burghers and, although Hans married up the social ladder, he made his own way in the mining industry as a smelter master, that is, a franchisee of copper companies that required an investment of his own money in the business. Martin was born and died in Eisleben, but his childhood was spent in the smaller mining town of Mansfeld where Hans and Margarete moved shortly after Martin's birth. Hans's business prospered and made him a prominent citizen. Recent excavations suggest that the Luther family ate well and lived comfortably in a large house built around a courtyard where Martin may have played with marbles found there and dated to the 1500s. Hans's fortune went up and down with the price of copper, but Martin and his siblings – at least one brother Jacob and three sisters who lived to adulthood – never knew real poverty. Jacob, with whom Martin was close, also became a smelter master and lived at the family's house after their father died.

Hans may have been the son of a peasant, but Martin himself always resided in towns and never, as far as we know, learned firsthand about rural life. Although he later complained that his schooling was hell and purgatory, the education Martin received, judged by his command of writing and speaking, prepared him well not only for the university but also for his work as teacher, author, translator, and preacher. Until the age of 14, he attended the Latin school in Mansfeld where he was drilled in grammar and taught the principles of logic and rhetoric. About 1497, together with a friend, Hans Reinecke, he was sent to the large city of Magdeburg, the residence of an archbishop, where in all likelihood they enrolled in the cathedral school. Luther lived with the Brothers of the Common Life, a non-cloistered, monastic-like community that took in pupils and sometimes tutored them. Magdeburg confronted a small-town boy with an intense urban and religious environment, but little is known about its impact because after one year Martin was sent to Eisenach to attend school in proximity to his mother's relatives. There, Luther boarded with Heinz Schalbe, a prominent citizen of the town and patron of the Franciscan monastery. With Schalbe's son, Caspar, he attended the school at St George's parish, and he developed a close friendship with John Braun, an elderly priest whom he later invited to his own first Mass. Luther could not know, of course, that 20 years after leaving Eisenach he would be hiding out at the Wartburg castle above the town.

For a talented student, the next step was the university, and in 1501 Luther chose Erfurt, a trading city 60 miles south of Mansfeld that had been prosperous enough in 1392 to establish its own university. Luther was to live in Erfurt for ten of the next eleven years, four at the university and six in the monastery. Like all beginning students, he matriculated in the faculty of liberal arts where he passed the baccalaureate exam in 1502. Preparing to become a master took longer and required the intense study of Aristotle. In early 1505, he finished second in a class of seventeen and received the symbols of a university teacher, a biretta and ring, which entitled him to give lectures and hold disputations. Moreover, he was now qualified to study in one of the professional faculties: jurisprudence, medicine, or theology. Following the plan of his father, for whom the study of law was the best path to a secure and prestigious career, Luther immediately embarked on the last stage of his education. It lasted less than two months. Returning to school after a visit home in July of 1505, Luther abruptly quit the study of law, gathered his astonished friends for a festive farewell, and was admitted to the Augustinian monastery nearby.

Piety appears to have been the decisive motive for this sudden change of course. Nearing Erfurt on his return, he was so terrified by a fierce storm that he vowed to become a monk if he escaped unscathed. To make such a life-changing vow, even in the face of death, Luther must have harboured misgivings about a law career and considered the possibility of a religious life in the strictest sense: the monastery. Besides, religion was everywhere he had lived and studied, especially in Magdeburg and Eisenach, and in Erfurt that teemed with churches, cloisters, and chapters of clergy. He could have studied theology without becoming a monk, but he was seeking not an alternate course of study but a different life.

As he looked back on that decision 40 years later, Luther recalled he had lived as a monk without reproach but still felt that he 'was a sinner before God with an extremely disturbed conscience'. This

AETHERNA IPSE SVAE MENTIS SIMVLACHRA LVTHERV
EXPRIMIT AT VVLTVS CERA LVCAE OCCIDVOS
·M·D·X·X·

1. Luther as a monk, by Lucas Cranach, 1520

evaluation of his 16 years as a monk was a common refrain. He tried to be a perfect monk, but his conscience was never soothed in spite of consolation offered by his mentor John von Staupitz, vicar-general of the observant (strict) Augustinians in Germany. His disquiet did not, however, hinder his advancement within the order. After completing the novitiate and making profession of his vows, Luther studied for the priesthood and was ordained on 3 April 1507, less than two years after he entered the order. One month later, he celebrated Mass for the first time. Accompanied by a party of 20 friends and relatives, Hans Luther came for the celebration and made a generous gift to the monastery. Nonetheless, Hans was not fully recovered from the disappointment caused by Luther's decision to become a monk. During their conversation, Luther insisted that his vow was not made freely but forced by extreme circumstances. Hans speculated that Luther had suffered an illusion and reminded his son of the Commandment to obey parents. When Luther recalled the meeting, he commented that nothing had ever cut to the quick and stayed with him so long as those words from the lips of his father.

After becoming a priest, Luther began the study of theology that lasted, with interruptions, until 1512, when he was awarded the doctorate and succeeded Staupitz as professor of theology at the new university in Wittenberg. At Erfurt, the Augustinians had their own school with teachers that also belonged to the university faculty. Even though Luther was already a master, he had to fulfil the requirements of a theology curriculum dominated by the scholastic method – so called because it was used in the 'schools' or universities. The standard textbook, compiled by Peter Lombard in the 12th century, was called the *Sentences* because it was constructed around debatable doctrinal statements for which Lombard provided arguments from older sources like Augustine. Every doctoral candidate in theology had to give lectures on the *Sentences* and many of them were revised and circulated as commentaries. In the 13th century, the young Thomas Aquinas had delivered such lectures, and Luther studied the *Sentences* commentary of Gabriel Biel, a brother of the common life who taught theology at the university of Tübingen and was still alive in Luther's childhood. Biel's approach to theology was called Nominalism, or Ockhamism after the 14th-century English Franciscan, William of Ockham. Since his primary Augustinian tutor in Erfurt was trained in this tradition, Luther also became, as he later acknowledged, an Ockhamist.

Unlike Aquinas, Ockhamist theologians emphasized that faith and doctrine depended more on revelation in scripture than on reason and natural knowledge. Although they drew a clear distinction between philosophy and theology, they still advocated both the study of Aristotle, which Luther had completed earlier, and of the Bible. Hence, Luther was able and willing to hold lectures on the *Ethics* of Aristotle as well as on the Bible and Lombard's *Sentences*. The lectures on Aristotle were delivered in 1508 and 1509 at Wittenberg, where Luther, probably at the behest of Staupitz, was a temporary replacement in the first of two positions allotted to the Augustinians: a lecturer in philosophy and a chair in theology filled by Staupitz. Luther remained in Wittenberg one year before returning to the Augustinian house in Erfurt and delivering his lectures on the *Sentences*. In late 1510, they were interrupted by the trip of his life – to Rome to make an appeal on behalf of the strict Augustinians.

The appeal was denied, but Rome made a deep impression on the earnest young monk who, as he later acknowledged, 'did not know the world at all'. He was both awed and disgusted by what he saw in the holy city and in towns along the way. Twenty years later, describing his 'pilgrimage to Rome' through the eyes of a reformer, he called himself a fanatical saint who 'dashed through all the churches and crypts believing all the stinking forgeries of those places'. At the time, he regretted that his parents were still alive because the Masses said in Rome, like indulgences offered there, were thought capable of redeeming them from purgatory. 'There is a saying in Rome: "Blessed is the mother whose son reads a

Mass on Saturday in St. John's." I should have liked to make my mother blessed, but it was too crowded and I could not get in; so I ate smoked herring instead.' Despite the flippant tone, Luther's words betray the sincerity of his monastic piety and priestly calling, a sincerity underlying later descriptions of his pre-Reformation self as an 'enthusiastic papist' and mired in 'monkery'.

By late 1511, Luther had been transferred to the Augustinian house in Wittenberg where he lived for the rest of his life, first as a monk and then as a husband and father. The next year he was installed in the only regularly paid position that he ever held: university professor. Staupitz persuaded Luther to take the doctor of theology degree and Elector Frederick agreed to pay the attached fees. It was a formality that concluded his study of theology and confirmed for Luther in Wittenberg the privileges of a university master earned in Erfurt. Professor Andrew Bodenstein, called Karlstadt after his home town, administered the oath in which Luther swore not to teach anything that was condemned by the church and offensive to pious ears. Besides another biretta and gold ring, he was given a closed and open Bible. As planned, Staupitz then surrendered his position on the faculty and Luther succeeded him in the chair of theology. This rapid series of events later became Luther's best defence against charges that he had no right to hold the opinions he did. As a publicly sworn doctor of theology, Luther argued that he was obligated to teach what he found in the Bible even when it was critical of church teaching and practice. Unknowingly, Staupitz had positioned Luther to start a reform movement that, as it turned out, Stauptiz could never bring himself to join.

For his first course, Luther chose a biblical book that was heard and sung every day in the monastery and that he knew almost by heart: the psalter. Since, however, he was treating the Psalms verse by verse as his medieval predecessors had done, he did not finish the course until 1515. Next, he devoted one year each to three

New Testament epistles: Romans, Galatians, and Hebrews. Those courses ended in 1518, the first full year of the indulgence controversy, which added extra travel and writing to his workload. Perhaps for that reason or because, as he said, he was better prepared the second time, he decided to lecture on the Psalms again, but the course was never completed. By the time he left for Worms in April of 1521, he had reached only Psalm 22. Besides lecturing at the university, Luther also had responsibilities within the order. Luther complained to his friend and brother Augustinian, John Lang, about how busy he was writing letters, preaching, supervising the study of other friars, lecturing on Paul, and visiting Augustinian houses as their district vicar.

At the university, Luther was also preparing theses for debate. One set, with ninety-eight theses, was critical of scholastic theology learned from his Nominalist teachers and Gabriel Biel. For most people, including the higher clergy, this theological debate was academic and therefore benign. Not so the second set of theses, also written in Latin and perhaps nailed to the door of the castle church in Wittenberg on 31 October 1517. If posted on that day, the eve of All Saints' Day, these Ninety-Five Theses on the power of indulgences would have greeted the crowds visiting the grandiose display of relics owned by Elector Frederick and hoping to obtain indulgences that would shorten their stay in purgatory. Indulgences were also being advertised as guarantees that the guilt of sin would be forgiven, albeit they only set aside the penalties imposed (penance) after sins were confessed to a priest. Years later, Luther would maintain that he never thought of going as far as he did: 'I intended only to attack indulgences; if anybody had said to me when I was at the Diet of Worms, "In a few years you will have a wife and your own household," I would not have believed it.' In fact, the Ninety-Five Theses attacked not only indulgence preachers but also the pope for allowing indulgences to be granted in exchange for money that was earmarked for the new basilica of St Peter in Rome. Some theses were brazen. 'It is vain', wrote Luther, 'to trust in salvation by indulgence letters even if the pope

Countless images have pictured Luther as a rebellious monk nailing the Ninety-Five Theses to the door of the castle church in Wittenberg on 31 October 1517. Luther himself never reported having engaged in that act of protest. The depiction of him posting the Theses stems from Philip Melanchthon, who was not present and who recorded the incident after Luther's death. In 1961, a posting of the Theses was called into question by the Roman Catholic historian, Erwin Iserloh. Iserloh's challenge elicited protests from Protestant scholars, and attempts are still being made to prove that Luther nailed the Theses even if they were meant only to announce a debate. In 2006, Martin Treu discovered a jotting (dated c. 1544) by George Rörer, Luther's secretary, which claimed that the Theses were posted by Luther on the doors 'of the churches' in Wittenberg on the eve of All Saints' Day 1517.

himself offered his soul as security.' Why doesn't the pope, he asked, build the basilica with his own money rather than with the money of poor believers? Christians should be taught that giving to the poor and needy was a better deed than buying an indulgence.

Luther's biting comments provoked trouble he did not expect. The Theses were forwarded to Rome by Archbishop Albert of Mainz, who was also profiting from the St Peter's indulgence offered in his domains. The issue of papal authority soon pushed indulgences into the background, and in 1518 Luther was summoned to Rome. At the request of Elector Frederick, Luther travelled instead to Augsburg where Cardinal Thomas Cajetan was instructed to obtain his recantation. Luther refused. When Cajetan demanded that Luther be turned over or driven out of Saxony, Elector Frederick refused and the die was cast. Pope Leo X issued a bull that confirmed papal teaching on indulgences and loyal theologians defended the divine origin of papal power. That topic was debated in 1519 at Leipzig by Luther and John Eck, who provoked the Wittenberger into his defence of Hus and became Luther's most tenacious opponent. At the beginning of 1520, Luther's case was reopened in Rome, and in June he was threatened with excommunication by a papal bull that was burned in December by Luther and his supporters. His formal excommunication followed quickly on 3 January 1521.

In the meantime, Luther had accumulated a broad range of support and a substantial body of writing in German and in Latin. German pamphlets on the sacraments and prayer quickly made him a popular religious author. Even the Ninety-Five Theses were circulated around Germany and read by clusters of Humanists who considered the indulgence trade an unsavoury way that Rome exploited pious Germans. In 1520, when Luther addressed this exploitation and other abuses in his *Address to the Christian Nobility*, political support grew. By that time, both faculty and Augustinian colleagues were also behind him. Karlstadt bought the entire edition of Augustine's works just published in Basel and provoked the Leipzig debate with 380 theses against Eck. Nicholas von Amsdorf, another early colleague who became a reformer, accompanied Luther and Karlstadt to Leipzig and was present at the Diet of Worms. In 1518, Philip Melancthon arrived in Wittenberg to teach Greek and soon became an admirer of Luther. Melanchthon was the most talented scholar of them all, a Humanist of the younger generation that supported the Reformation.

In addition to the backing that came from external sources, Martin Luther became a reformer because of two realizations that emerged from his own life and study. One happened prior to the Diet of Worms and one came afterwards at the Wartburg. The first realization became the theological underpinning of reform and is commonly called his 'reformation discovery', although Luther did not report it in detail until the year before he died. According to that flashback, after many attempts Luther finally perceived what Paul meant when he wrote to the Romans (1:17) that the righteousness or justice of God was revealed in the gospel and not in the law. Since the preceding verse defined the gospel, literally 'good news', as the power of God that saved believers, Luther could not comprehend how God's justice could be bad news, that is, the threatening standard of righteousness he had tried unsuccessfully to meet. The problem was not only theological but also personal, and its solution seemed like a new birth:

> I began to understand that the righteousness of God meant that those who were righteous lived by a gift of God, which is the passive righteousness by which God justifies us through faith, as it is written: 'They who through faith are righteous shall live' (Habakkuk 2:4). I felt I was altogether born again and had entered paradise through open gates.

The faith in question was trust in God's promises that were fulfilled in Jesus the Messiah. Since this faith replaced fasting, pilgrimages, prayers to saints, special Masses, and other ways that medieval believers made themselves righteous or acceptable to God, Luther's insight undermined not only the reigning theology but also most of the piety that characterized medieval Christianity.

Old biographies of Luther referred to his realization of what Paul meant by gospel as Luther's 'tower experience', because it may have occurred in the tower of the Augustinian house in Wittenberg. In *Table Talk*, Luther located his realization both in the tower and in the 'cl.' of the monastery. Some scholars, especially those favouring a psychoanalytical interpretation, read cl. as *cloaca*, or toilet, and reconstructed a scene which connected Luther's realization with both physical and emotional release. Recent research has abandoned the notion of a tower experience in any but the most general terms. At the end of his flashback, Luther emphasized how long and hard he had worked at understanding scripture and not how suddenly he found the answer. *Cloaca* may have been a disparaging metaphor for earthly existence in general or for the torment of living without hope of pleasing God.

The second realization was described in a letter with which Luther dedicated to his father a lengthy rejection of monastic vows. Composed at the Wartburg in November 1521, the letter resolved for Martin the regret he felt over upsetting his father's plans for a good marriage and career by deciding to become a monk. The unpleasant meeting between them after his first Mass had weighed on Luther's mind but now, he wrote, he realized that his father's disappointment was only the expression of care for a son he loved and that, moreover, his father had been right: he, Martin, should have obeyed the fourth Commandment to honour parents. Since his father could not, however, drag Luther out of the monastery, God stepped in, liberated him, and made out of Luther a new creature, 'not of the pope but of Christ'. That was not all. Luther also believed he was called to lead a movement that would bring to other children the same freedom that he now experienced. To his father, Luther expressed it this way:

> I hope that [Christ] has snatched one son from you in order that through me he might begin to help many other children of his; and I am convinced that you will not only willingly allow this, as you ought, but also rejoice at it with great joy!

Impelled by this calling, Luther defied Elector Frederick and returned to Wittenberg to assume leadership of a nascent reform movement that became the European Reformation.

Chapter 3
The labours of reform

Luther returned to Wittenberg on 6 March 1522, the same day on which the town council decided to give him a bolt of cloth for new monastic garb. In accord with the ambivalence expressed four months earlier in the phrase 'still a monk and yet not a monk', Luther wore the monastic habit until 1524 while becoming simultaneously the leader of the evangelical movement. He had no illusion of achieving reform by himself. In a letter from the Wartburg, Luther had urged Melanchthon and other colleagues to take their message beyond Wittenberg:

> You lecture, Amsdorf lectures; Jonas will lecture; do you want the kingdom of God to be proclaimed only in your town? Do not others also need the gospel? Will your Antioch not release a Silas or a Paul or a Barnabas for some other work of the Spirit?

The references to prominent missionaries in the Acts of the Apostles and the comparison of Wittenberg to Antioch showed that Luther envisioned the reformation as a missionary enterprise to be directed from Wittenberg, where his leadership had to be reasserted and defined. On 9 March 1522, Luther preached in the town church the first of eight sermons that described how he would change the pace and direction of reform which had been set by his colleague Karlstadt. The Invocavit sermons (named after the first Sunday of Lent in the liturgical calendar) argued for greater sympathy with laity who were offended and confused by sudden changes in worship and piety. For the time being, that sympathy demanded a slower pace of reform. Karlstadt vigorously defended his actions but had little choice but to cede the initiative to Luther.

Luther did not intend to tarry unduly. According to his theology of history, the reforming moment had to be seized: God's word and grace had always been like a passing shower of rain, he wrote, which never returned to a place it had been. Between 1522 and 1530, that sense of urgency forced him and the colleagues in Wittenberg to find answers to critical questions. How quickly should private Masses be abolished, both elements given to the laity, and a new public liturgy adopted in the parishes? How should marriage be defined and regulated now that clerical celibacy was no longer required and episcopal courts were no longer available to settle disputes? To what extent should Christians obey civil authority now that princes and city councils were defying the emperor and supporting the reformation? Should monastic vows be forbidden and what provision should be made for monks and nuns who did not leave their cloisters? How should laity handle personal and business affairs when the end of the world, as Luther supposed, was so near at hand? To answer the last question, Luther appealed to the Sermon on the Mount and concluded that Christians should not charge interest. On the issue of civil conduct, however, Luther was more pragmatic and tempered the teaching of Jesus ('do not resist evil') with the thirteenth chapter of Romans that enjoined obedience to rulers. True Christians, he wrote, have no need of government for they would neither do evil nor resist it done to them. He realized, however, that few believers led an ideal Christian life and therefore civil authority was necessary to keep evil in check. In 1523, Luther admonished communities, out of Christian love and not merely out of civic duty, to redirect the wealth of clerical chapters and monasteries to poor relief, evangelical preaching, and education.

The course of events forced Luther's hand and led him to take controversial stands. The peasants' revolt of 1525 placed him in a most difficult spot. On the one hand, he pronounced the grievances of the common folk to be just but, on the other, he rejected the violence employed by them to achieve their goals. When he defended the harsh means used by his prince and others to suppress the revolution, he was denounced as a lackey of the rulers. After the Ottoman Turks crushed a Christian army in Hungary in 1526 and besieged Vienna in 1529, Luther argued that Christians could be soldiers and that war against the Turks was justified, as long as the war was not a crusade and soldiers understood they were only defending neighbours and loved ones. In *Freedom of a Christian*, written in late 1520 and sent to Pope Leo X not long before Leo excommunicated him, Luther described ideal Christians as people whose faith made them the freest lords of all, subject to no one and whose love made them the most dutiful servants of all subject to everyone. Applying this template to the unforeseen conflicts of the 1520s was, however, a thorny challenge.

Throughout the decade, Luther was also occupied with divisions both inside and outside his own circle. The challenges came from Karlstadt, Ulrich Zwingli, and the Anabaptists, each of whom interpreted and practised the sacraments in ways Luther could not accept. After Karlstadt left Wittenberg, he surrendered his university status and settled in the town of Orlamünde to transform it into the kind of Christian community he had envisioned for Wittenberg. He stopped baptizing infants and celebrated, in German and without vestments, a simple communion service. In pamphlets directed at Luther, he formulated a spiritual theology which denied that salvation once gained on the cross had to be mediated through sacraments. In turn, Luther defended preaching and sacraments as external means of God's grace, through which the treasures of the cross were publicly and personally conveyed. Karlstadt also argued that the words of Jesus which instituted the Lord's Supper did not literally mean that the communion bread was the body of Christ and the wine his blood. On this point, Zwingli, Luther's counterpart in Zurich, also departed from Luther's belief that Christ was really present in the bread and wine. In Zwingli's view, Jesus intended for his words to be understood spiritually and figuratively: the bread and the wine only signified his body and blood that were offered on the cross for the salvation of all. The sacrament was a spiritual oneness with the cross, but it contained no mysterious physical reception of Christ and no salvation was imparted through it. In 1529, when they met at Marburg for the only time, Zwingli and Luther could find no agreement on this issue, and their rift led to a permanent division between Reformed and Lutheran branches of the Protestant Reformation.

The two reformers were united, however, in their opposition to Anabaptists who broke with Zwingli in 1525 over the pace of reform in Zurich. For his critics, Zwingli was too cautious, and infant baptism, which his radical followers deemed unbiblical, was the culprit that kept the church coterminous with the city and subject to its magistrates. In 1528, Luther published a rejection of believers' baptism in which he praised infant baptism as a fine feature of pre-Reformation Christianity. To make baptism depend upon a deliberate decision to believe based salvation upon the shifting sand of human choice and underestimated God's grace. The limitation of human choice was also Luther's argument against the Humanist Erasmus, who attacked Luther's denial of free will in matters of grace and salvation. In a 1525 treatise entitled *The Bound Will*, Luther argued that the power of sin held the human will in its sway before the Holy Spirit liberated it to trust God. After baptism the believer was still dependent on the Spirit's power to keep faith alive and prevent the will from falling back into sin. At stake for Luther was the essence of Christianity that he called the gospel: the only way to salvation was faith in Christ and that faith was a gift of the Spirit, not a free choice made by a neutral will, which for Luther did not exist. The same concern was behind Luther's debates with Catholic opponents over private Masses, pilgrimages, fasting, indulgences, monastic vows, clerical celibacy, giving alms, and praying to saints.

They were touted as supplements to faith or 'good works', which the free human will could use to please God and earn salvation more easily than by faith alone. Luther and his colleagues felt it necessary to discard or modify those works, but they also had to provide new ways in which believers could nurture and express their faith.

A ready impetus was supplied by the rapid expansion of the Wittenberg reformation within Germany and beyond to Eastern Europe and Scandinavia. When a town or territory became Protestant, civil authorities would ban the medieval Mass in favour of a Lutheran service of worship, withdraw from the jurisdiction of Catholic bishops, allow priests, monks, and nuns to marry, and prohibit publicly most of the old piety. These measures were codified for each principality in new religious constitutions that were called church orders. Luther's colleague, John Bugenhagen, assumed much of that responsibility in northern Germany and Denmark. In and around Saxony, the peasants' revolt left in its wake neglected parishes and confused pastors who needed both guidance and fresh materials with which to turn their flocks into Protestants. Luther himself provided the most essential manuals: postils or guides to preaching on biblical texts, a evangelical order of worship in the *German Mass* (1526), hymns, translations of scripture, and catechisms (both large and small, 1529) that explained for laity and clergy the Ten Commandments, the Creed, the Lord's Prayer, and the sacraments. A provisional church order was written for Saxony by Melanchthon and Luther in 1528. It was used by teams of inspectors to assess the condition of Saxon parishes and to advise pastors how to teach the evangelical message and to reorganize the church.

In 1530, the Coburg fortress on the southern edge of Saxony sheltered Luther, the imperial outlaw, during the Diet of Augsburg at which Emperor Charles V rejected the statements of faith he had sought from German and Swiss reformers. The 28 articles submitted by the Wittenbergers and their allies, commonly called the Augsburg Confession, became the founding document of churches that gradually used the name 'Lutheran' to distinguish their expanding movement from Rome and from the Reformed Protestant churches emerging in Zurich and Geneva. The addition of ducal Saxony (the half of Saxony that had remained loyal to Rome) to the growing list of Lutheran territories brought tremendous satisfaction to the Wittenbergers. In 1539, Luther marked the occasion with a sermon in Leipzig, where 20 years earlier he and Karlstadt had debated John Eck under the hostile eyes of Catholic Duke George. Luther opened the sermon, delivered on a Saturday, with the admission that he did not feel well and needed to stick closely to the gospel lesson appointed for the next day, which happened to be the festival of Pentecost. The text (John 14:23–31) began with the assurance that Jesus and his Father would make their home with all those who heard the word of Jesus and kept it. Luther found comfort in the text, but he also found a definition of the true church (those who kept the word of Jesus) to contrast with the pope and his church, which he found plenty of energy to denounce. The next afternoon he preached in the church of St Thomas, later made famous by Bach, and on Monday he departed for home in the company of Jonas, Melanchthon, and the new Protestant Duke Henry, who escorted them for the first 20 miles.

The journey to Leipzig was a high point of his later years but also typical of the short trips he made to destinations near Wittenberg during the 1530s. Except for 1535, he made one or more of these trips every year in spite of the fact that he suffered periodically from temporary ailments. Most of the journeys, like visits to the other residences of Elector John Frederick, had a political agenda, but in October of 1538 he accompanied Jonas and Erasmus Spiegel, captain of the guard in Wittenberg, on a short hunting trip. While Spiegel was pursuing a hare, his horse fell and died, and Luther speculated the hare must have been a spectre of Satan. When he was summoned back to Wittenberg because the elector wanted to see him, Luther was reluctant to leave because Jonas had been seized with an attack of kidney stones. At home, Luther was receiving a stream of prominent visitors, including Martin Bucer, Wolfgang Capito, and their colleagues from southern Germany, who were seeking agreement on the Lord's Supper in order to strengthen the Protestant alliance. Owing to his poor health, Luther had asked them to come to Wittenberg, but when they arrived, he at first showed little inclination to negotiate. Surprisingly, however, a genuine agreement was reached that required little or no compromise on either side. Luther accepted Bucer's statement that the body and blood of Christ were present and offered to the faithful with the bread and wine; and both Bucer and Luther agreed that 'unworthy' recipients received the body and blood of Christ, although they may have harboured different meanings of 'unworthy'. The theologians declared themselves to be brothers and celebrated the Lord's Supper together. The result of the agreement was not a unified Protestant front since the Swiss did not accept it, but it did enable more south Germans who had wavered between Zwingli and Luther to ally themselves with the north German Lutherans.

In late 1535, the papal nuncio, Vergerio, had arrived in Wittenberg to sound out Luther about the papal intention to call a council. Breakfasting with Bugenhagen and Luther at the castle, a curious Vergerio also inquired about their church practices like ordaining priests, and Luther assured him that ordinations of pastors had been resumed even though no bishops were available to perform them. The trio engaged in friendly banter and Luther promised to attend the council if it were held. In 1536, Pope Paul III did invoke a council to begin the next year in Mantua, and both rulers and theologians met in February 1537 at Schmalkald to decide if they should send delegates to the council. A summons to the council presented by the papal legate was impolitely refused by Elector John Frederick, who had remained steadfastly against Protestant attendance despite Luther's advice to the contrary. Luther remembered the meeting all too well because he was afflicted by a severe urinary blockage that resisted medical treatment until it finally yielded on his way home. His suffering at Schmalkald was so acute that theological discussions had to be interrupted and everyone feared he might die. His party, returning carefully by way of Erfurt and Weimar, took two weeks to reach Wittenberg.

EFFIGIES PHIL: MELANCHTHONIS · ANN · AET ·
XXX CZ LVCA CRONACHIO PICTORE ·
· M · D · XXXVII ·

2. Philip Melanchthon, by Lucas Cranach, 1537

Back in Wittenberg, he resumed a full schedule of writing, lecturing, preaching, and serving as dean of the theological faculty, while other friends and colleagues, like Melanchthon, Bugenhagen, Jonas, and Amsdorf attended to matters of reform elsewhere. Two of the main sources for his theology are still the lectures on Galatians delivered in 1531 (published 1535, 1538) and the course on Genesis that commenced in 1535 and lasted for a decade. Addressing a younger generation of students, Luther felt he had to remind them why the Reformation was necessary and how important it was to protect what had been achieved. In 1538, he gave similar reasons for working hard to his former Augustinian brother and student, James Propst, now a reformer in Bremen. Even though he was 'an exhausted, old man tired out from so many labours', he became younger every day because new sects were always rising up against him. Six years later, Luther took pleasure in dedicating a newly built chapel at the residence of his own Saxon ruler in Torgau. One of the earliest churches built specifically as a Lutheran place of worship, the chapel was designed around the pulpit to emphasize preaching as the centre of worship. Its clean lines were decorated with paintings from the workshop of Luther's friend, Lucas Cranach; on the end wall above the table for the Lord's Supper was mounted an organ for the music of Johann Walther, the cantor of the Saxon electors and composer of early Reformation music. Luther asserted that Jesus had given his followers the freedom to assemble for worship when and where it was most convenient; in that spirit the chapel at the castle was not a special church for the court but rather a place of worship for any and all who wanted to come. In fact, he said, one could preach just as well outside by the fountain.

The fear of losing it all was behind the strident tone that marked many of his late writings. In 1544, Luther admonished a colleague to pray without ceasing for the church because it faced great danger. On the one hand, some fear was justified. In the 1540s, the Catholic Council of Trent signalled the earnest intention of Rome to reform itself and Emperor Charles V ran out of patience and

3. Pulpit in the Lutheran church at the Torgau Castle, 1544

decided to force German Protestants back under the pope. On the other hand, Luther exaggerated the threats posed by his opponents, whom he lumped under one label as enemies of the gospel. He denounced Turks, Jews, papists, and 'sacramentarians' (Protestants opposed to his sacramental views) as agents of the devil intent on destroying the truth recovered by the Lutheran movement. The repeated advances of the Ottoman Turks into Central Europe did cause genuine anxiety, but the unease felt by Luther and other reformers at the Jewish presence in Europe was irrational. This unease came from their naïve disappointment that Jews had not been persuaded by the evangelical message to convert in large numbers and from the anti-Jewish climate of late medieval Europe that had already led to persecution and expulsions. In 1546, as he did in 1521, Luther regarded the Reformation as a divine work and himself as God's agent in a mighty struggle with the devil.

Early in the morning of 18 February 1546, Luther died in Eisleben, the same town in which he was born, after successfully mediating a dispute among the counts of Mansfeld. He was lodging in a house that had belonged to Dr Philip Drachstedt, like Luther's father a prominent smelter master in Mansfeld, who had also studied law and become a court councillor. According to witnesses, his friend Justus Jonas and the pastor at Mansfeld, Michael Coelius, Luther died peacefully after confessing his faith. Before the body was returned to Wittenberg, a likeness of Luther's face was cast in wax and sketches were made for posthumous portraits. Luther was interred near the pulpit in the castle church after a sermon by Bugenhagen and the eulogy by Melanchthon, who told the mourners 'we are very much like orphans deprived of a fine and faithful father'. Earlier, Melanchthon had announced Luther's death to his students by alluding to the ascension of Elijah in a fiery chariot (2 Kings 2:12): 'The charioteer of Israel who guided the church in these last days of the world is gone.'

Chapter 4
Luther's Bible

Martin Luther would never have called the Bible his own; yet there are good reasons for naming this chapter 'Luther's Bible'. He spent more time on this book than any other, and the translation into German made by Luther and his colleagues (still called the *Lutherbibel*) has remained a cultural emblem for almost 500 years. Luther's own translation of the New Testament, completed within three months at the Wartburg, was a bestseller in its day. After being published in September 1522 – and known therefore as his 'September Testament' – the printing of 3,000 to 5,000 copies sold out in three months. A new edition was issued in December, and during the next 12 years over 100 more editions appeared. Prior to 1534, when the complete Wittenberg Bible appeared, around 200,000 copies of Luther's New Testament had been disseminated.

For all that, Luther never considered his translation to be the only legitimate version. He did not scorn the assistance of other scholars or discourage them from making their own translations. After the Greek edition and Latin version of the New Testament by Erasmus appeared in 1516 and 1519, Luther made use of it for his own study and translating. From his refuge at the Wartburg in late 1521, he wrote to his Augustinian brother John Lang:

I will stay hidden in this place until Easter. Meanwhile, I plan to write the postil and to translate the new testament into the vernacular, which our friends desire. I hear that you are doing the same thing. Keep on as you have begun. Oh that every city had its own translator and that this book could be found in all languages, hands, eyes, ears, and hearts!

The postil mentioned by Luther refers to the reading and preaching guides on the appointed biblical texts for Sundays and festivals of the church year. Luther kept his word and the first three sets, for Advent and Christmas, appeared in 1521 and 1522. Before his death, seven more sets of postils, some of which contained duplicates, revisions, and material not from Luther's pen, were edited and published. Luther did not intend them to be model sermons; they varied considerably in style and length, and were not suitable for reading to a congregation. Some short passages, however, are imaginative and vivid, like the following comment by Luther on the Christmas story:

When [Mary and Joseph] came to Bethlehem, they were very insignificant and despised people. They were obliged to make room for everybody until they were shown into a stable and had to share with the animals a common hostel, table, and bed. Meanwhile, inside the inn many a rogue occupied the seat of honour and was treated as a gentleman. Nobody noticed or understood what God was performing in the stable. He permitted the big houses and expensive rooms to remain empty; he allowed them to eat, drink, and to be of good cheer, but this solace and treasure [in the manger] was hidden from them. How dark the night over Bethlehem must have been that they could not see such light.

Luther also knew much of the Bible by heart, especially the Psalms chanted by him and the other monks every day. His lectures on books of the Bible over the course of 34 years are full of cross-references to biblical passages that he quoted from memory but not always exactly as they were found in Hebrew,

Greek, Latin, or German. In fact, when translating, Luther was not above adding a word to the original text in order to enhance the meaning of a passage. A conspicuous and controversial example was his addition of the word 'alone' to the text of Romans 3:28: 'For we hold that person is justified by faith [alone] apart from works prescribed by the law.' Responding to criticism of this addition, Luther argued that it not only conveyed the sense of the text but was also good German and made the translation clearer and more vigorous. A translation should speak German, not Greek or Latin, and a translator should not ask the Latin text how to speak good German but instead be guided by 'the mother in the home, children on the street, and ordinary people in the marketplace'.

Although it was not always translated literally, the biblical text was still taken seriously. Luther rejected the notion that scripture was like a 'waxen nose' or a 'bending reed' that could be manipulated to prop up personal opinions. Enhancing the native meaning of a Greek or Hebrew passage by making it speak German was different from importing a foreign meaning into the passage because it suited the translator's views. When the Hebrew or Greek was difficult, however, and early manuscripts in those languages did not agree, the exact meaning of a passage could be elusive. To find it, Luther did not rely on his linguistic ability alone, not even while translating the New Testament, a task that he acknowledged was 'beyond his strength'. In addition to Erasmus's Latin version, he consulted at least one or two of the eighteen German Bibles that were already in print by 1522. Before he returned to Wittenberg, Luther sent part of his translation to Spalatin, who sent it on to Melanchthon, the new professor of Greek, with whom Luther polished the first draft between his return in March and the publication of the German New Testament in September.

More collegiality was in evidence during the translation of the Old Testament. During the 1520s, Luther was part of a team that included Melanchthon and Matthew Aurogallus, who had come to Wittenberg in 1521 to teach Hebrew and arrived just in time to work on the translation. Both Melanchthon and Aurogallus knew Hebrew better than Luther did, but his skill had increased while lecturing twice on the Psalms and preparing a translation and explanation of the seven penitential Psalms that appeared in 1517. Translating the Old Testament proved to be a slow process even for a team of scholars. The Book of Job was so difficult that only three lines could be translated every four days, and some books of the Old Testament appeared by themselves before they were incorporated into the full German Bible published at Wittenberg in 1534. By that time, the entire psalter had appeared in several editions, the best of which was published in 1531 after the team had met 16 afternoons and evenings to make final revisions. Defending that translation, Luther reported that 'we have at times translated quite literally – even though we could have rendered the meaning more clearly another way – because everything turns on the very words'. As an example, he offered the phrase 'you have ascended on high; you have led captivity captive' (Psalm 68:18), which the church's liturgy had connected to the ascension of Christ. According to Luther, good German would have prescribed the reading, 'you have set the captives free', but that did not 'convey the fine, rich meaning of the Hebrew', which suggested that Christ not only freed the slaves but also defeated the captive power of sin and brought eternal redemption.

The first complete German Bible was printed in 1534 at the workshop of Hans Lufft in Wittenberg. Of the 12 additional printings issued by Lufft prior to 1546, the 1541 edition underwent the most thorough revision by Luther and his team. Most of the credit went to Luther both before and after his death. Soon after the first edition appeared, the reformer Anton Corvinus expressed his excitement at the appearance of a German Bible translated better than ever before 'by you, my dear Luther'. At his funeral, Melanchthon's eulogy praised the reformer for turning the scriptures into German with such clarity that they would bring to

4. The Old and New Testaments. Title page of the *Biblia Germanica*, 1545

future readers more light than many commentaries could do. The complete Bible also contained Luther's prefaces to the Old and New Testaments, the Apocrypha, and to various books within each Testament and the Apocrypha. These prefaces contain many of his finest comments about reading and interpreting the scripture, and they were available to everyone who opened the Bible. In the margins, a user would also find pithy comments by Luther that defended his translation and offered explanations of the text. The workshop of Lucas Cranach contributed over 120 woodcut illustrations, which appear beautifully hand-coloured in the 2003 two-volume facsimile version.

The phrase 'Luther's Bible' also has relevance for understanding the way he interpreted scripture and viewed its authority. Luther inherited a medieval scheme for extracting different levels of meaning from a passage, but he did not apply it consistently. On occasion, he would adopt an allegorical explanation, but he hovered mostly between literal and spiritual interpretations, the latter being most evident when he argued, like New Testament writers, that passages in Hebrew scripture pointed to Jesus the messiah. This interpretation of the Old Testament was a venerable way of treating both Testaments as one sacred scripture, but it gave no specific directions about how Christians should react to commands from the Old Testament like those in Leviticus. Luther's general answer was clean and simple. Where the Old Testament offered divine promises of mercy and redemption, it should be honoured and applied to Christ. Where it offered examples of faith and unfaith, it should be heeded. When it gave commands and laws, the reader should ask whether or not they applied to Christians and 'use them as we please to our advantage'. With the Christian tradition, however, Luther believed the Ten Commandments agreed with natural law and provided a 'mirror of life' in which everyone could see wherein they were lacking. The decalogue provided the texts for a number of Luther's sermons and his explanations of the Ten Commandments comprised the first part of his catechisms.

The touchstone of his biblical interpretation was the gospel, which he defined 'at its briefest' as 'a discourse about Christ, that he is the son of God and became human for us, that he died and was raised, that he has been established as Lord over all things'. The gospel was 'our guide and instructor in the scriptures', which Luther used to rate the usefulness of books in both Testaments. In his preface to the New Testament, he ranked the gospel of John and the epistles of Paul and Peter above the other books: they showed Christ and taught everything that was necessary to know about salvation. In that same preface, Luther called the letter of James an 'epistle of straw' because it had nothing of the gospel about it. Despite this notorious comment, Luther was not prepared to remove James from the Bible; the specific preface to James and Jude praised the book because it vigorously proclaimed the law of God and contained many good sayings. Luther did not, however, believe James was written by an apostle nor could he number it among the chief books. Accordingly, the table of contents for the 1522 German New Testament separated James and three others – Hebrews, Jude, and Revelation – from the first 23 books by a large space at the bottom of the page. It was the most vivid illustration of Luther's oft-quoted statement: 'All the genuine sacred books agree in this, that all of them preach and inculcate Christ.'

For so much conviction and apparent certainty about how to interpret the Bible, Luther could at times be quite diffident and flexible. When his earliest lectures on Galatians were published after much revision, he sent them to Staupitz with the following commentary:

> Reverend Father, I am sending you two copies of my foolish Galatians. I am not as pleased with it as I was at first, and I see that it could have been explained more clearly and completely, but who can do everything at once? In fact, who can manage to produce very much on a regular basis? Nevertheless, I am confident that Paul is made clearer here than he has been before, though it is not yet satisfactory to my taste.

In 1521, Luther made a similar comment to Elector Frederick about his lectures on the first 22 Psalms that he called a work in progress. Admitting that he did not know whether or not he had always discovered the correct interpretation, he maintained that no commentator, however renowned, had ever exhausted the meaning of a Psalm. Every interpreter of the Bible fell short, although some were better than others. In the Psalms, Luther was seeing things that Augustine did not see, and after him others would see things that Luther had not found. The only recourse was for interpreters to be of mutual help to one another and to forgive those who were found wanting, since everyone, including Luther, would eventually fall short. In fact, who would dare to assert that anyone had completely understood just one Psalm? Our life, said Luther here and elsewhere, 'is one of beginning and of growth, not one of consummation'. In his preface to volume one of his 1539 collected German works, Luther summarized his approach to the Bible in three words that betrayed his monastic formation: prayer, meditation, and trial (*oratio*, *meditatio*, *tentatio*). Before interpreting a passage, one should pray to the Spirit for guidance, fix the words of the text in one's mind through meditation, and not shun either personal distress or attacks by others. Trials would teach you 'not only to know and understand but also to experience how right, how true, how sweet, how lovely, how mighty, how comforting God's word is, wisdom beyond all wisdom'. Luther had in mind his own experience with the papacy and its theologians. He claimed to be 'deeply indebted' to them for pounding, oppressing, and harrowing him so much that they made him a 'fairly good theologian', which otherwise he would not have become.

Those remarks made the authority of scripture appear quite subjective and it was. 'Scripture alone' (*sola scriptura*), which for some became the motto of the Protestantism, never meant for Luther that the Bible was the exclusive authority on every issue or that it offered a clear-cut, objective answer to every question. It did mean that on matters of dispute in the church it was the chief authority. The formula 'scripture alone' arose in Luther's conflict with the papacy as a statement of the Bible's superiority over the opinions of earlier theologians, the rules of canon law, and the decrees of councils and of popes. At one time or another, both sides called on all these authorities. Defending his position before Cardinal Cajetan in 1518, Luther cited statements by Augustine and Bernard of Clairvaux in addition to passages of scripture. For Luther, however, the decisive evidence came from scripture: 'Divine truth, that is scripture, is master over the pope and I do not await human judgement when I have learned the judgement of God.' In his debate with John Eck in 1519, the words of Jesus to Peter in Matthew 16 and John 20 – as Luther interpreted them – were the crucial evidence in his case against the divine origin of the papacy. At Worms, Luther concluded his speech with an appeal not only to scripture but to convincing arguments and to his conscience. What was the real authority here: scripture, rational argumentation, or Luther's conscience? The correct answer is all of the above. On those points that concerned the source and process of salvation, Luther believed the Bible was absolutely clear, but he also knew that good arguments had to be made for that clarity on every disputed issue in order for the conscience to take a stand with integrity. For the reformer, the authority of scripture had both subjective and objective components.

Of equal importance with the authority of scripture was the principle of Christian freedom that he explained with eloquent simplicity in his 1520 essay of the same title and in the 1522 sermons at Wittenberg. Christian freedom meant that – according to scripture – nothing besides faith in Christ could be made a condition of salvation or imposed on believers. The Reformation would have no purpose if the Bible were wielded as a paper pope to dethrone and replace the primate of Rome. Some policies and regulations were necessary, as Luther and his colleagues learned while organizing new evangelical churches. The chief principle on which such policies should be based was not,

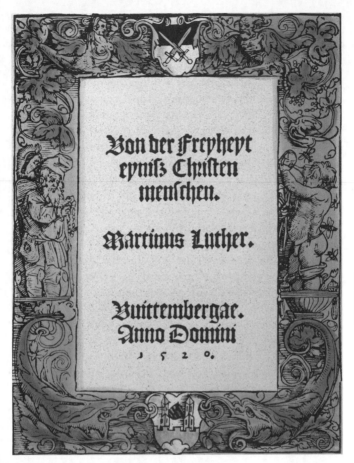

5. Title page, *Freedom of a Christian*, 1520

however, the literal following of biblical verses and customs but
the facilitation and protection of Christian freedom. In Luther's
own blunt formulation: 'I teach that people should trust in
nothing but Jesus Christ alone, not in prayers or merits or even in
their own works.' For other Protestants, scripture may have been
the chief authority *per se*, but not for Luther; it was an authority

because its story of promise and redemption defined and insisted upon Christian freedom.

It was a broad concept of authority, and Luther's hermeneutical principles were flexible, a mixture of things that modern interpreters tend to keep separate: what a text could have meant in the past and what it could or should mean today. Sometimes he would apply a biblical statement literally to his 16th-century classroom or congregation, and other times he would dismiss a passage because it belonged to yesterday and had no direct relevance for today. In fact, 'today' (*hodie* in Latin) was one of his favourite words in sermons and in lectures which often sounded like sermons. To a large extent, Luther lived in the world of the Bible. His calendar was the church year, his history was the sacred history of redemption and its fulfilment at the last day, his mentors were patriarchs, prophets, apostles, and teachers throughout church history, his church the flock of believers scattered throughout the world. And his Bible was a book of the church. Contrary to popular lore, Luther did not believe that people in isolation could interpret the Bible any way they wished and then impose that interpretation upon others in church and society. He lived before people could buy their own Bibles and use them as independent sources of God's word that sufficed without the church. Luther could not imagine that scenario, even though the printing press and translations by himself and other reformers eventually made that scenario a reality. The last words attributed to him directly contradicted that severance of the Bible from the church:

> No one can presume to have tasted the scriptures sufficiently unless that person has ruled over the church with the prophets for a thousand years. We are beggars, that is true.

Chapter 5
The new Christianity

Like other reformers, Martin Luther failed to find in the Bible many features of the piety practised by believers around him. One of those features – acquiring indulgences in order to avoid doing penance for sin and to reduce one's tenure in purgatory – was the object of his criticism in the Ninety-Five Theses that ignited the Reformation. By the time he was excommunicated four years later, Luther was proposing an alternate way of practising Christianity that was based on what he believed had been neglected or distorted by late medieval religion. His Christianity was not completely new, of course. In 1540, when he was challenged by more radical reformers, he admitted:

> We on our part confess that much is Christian and good under the papacy; indeed everything that is Christian and good is to be found there and has come from that source. For instance,...the true holy scriptures, true baptism, the true sacrament of the altar, the true keys to the forgiveness of sins, the true office of the ministry, the true catechism in the form of the Lord's prayer, the ten commandments, and the articles of the creed.

Why then did he criticize the Roman Church and regard the pope as the Antichrist?

> Because [the pope] does not keep to these treasures of Christendom, which he has inherited from the apostles. He

makes additions of the devil and does not use these treasures
for the improvement of the temple. Instead, he works toward its
destruction by setting his commandments above the ordinance of
Christ. But Christ preserves his Christendom even in the midst of
such destruction.... In fact both remain: the antichrist sits in the
temple of God (2 Thessalonians 2:3–4), while the temple still is and
remains the temple of God through the power of Christ.

Luther had no intention of starting a new church. His agenda,
once it crystallized after his decision to become a reformer, was to
recover the authentic Christianity that had been lost. Nonetheless,
Luther's agenda contained enough revolutionary changes in piety
and practice for some clergy and laity to resist them. Those who
did become Protestant would practise a Christianity that was new
to them because it was not their ancestors' religion.

Luther's attitude towards the Marian piety of the late Middle Ages
was typical of his agenda. He rejected any rituals and titles used in
Marian devotion that infringed on the role of her son: she was not
a co-redeemer with Jesus and she was not the merciful mother
who sheltered believers from a harsh judgement. The title 'queen
of heaven' was true in a sense, but 'it did not make her a goddess
who could grant gifts or render aid, as some suppose when they
pray and flee to her rather than to God'. The ancient title 'mother
of God' was, however, the greatest thing a believer could say of her.
Whoever would honour Mary must not isolate her, he cautioned,

but set her in the presence of God and far beneath God, strip her of
all honour and regard her 'low estate' (Luke 1:48), then marvel at
the exceedingly abundant grace of God, who regards, embraces, and
blesses so despised a mortal.... She does not want you to come to
her, but through her to God.

Luther did not contest Mary's status as the patron saint of the
town church in Wittenberg or seek to remove two depictions of
the Madonna from the church's west portal. According to one

source, a picture of the Madonna adorned one wall of his study and inspired the following remark: 'The child sleeps on Mary's arm; one day he will wake up and ask us how we have conducted ourselves.' Luther recognized a legitimate tradition of Marian devotion within Christianity that needed to be purged of the excesses it had accrued.

These excesses and other medieval 'additions' were often targeted by him. In a sermon from the early 1530s, Luther identified the 'evildoers' and false prophets of Matthew 7:22–23 as his Roman opponents and described why he refuted them:

> You are showing me your teachings and signs, which point me to rosaries, pilgrimages, the worship of saints, masses, monkery, and other special and self-chosen works. There is nothing here about Christ, or about faith, baptism, and the sacrament [of the altar], or about good works which Christ teaches me to practise, within my station, in relation to my neighbour.

This accusation by Luther not only specifies 'additions' to be rejected; it also restates the 'treasures' that he wanted to purify and preserve: the centrality of Christ alone, the right kind of faith and good works, and the proper use of the sacraments. Taking each of these in turn will illustrate the renewed Christianity that Luther wanted to recover for Germany.

The first of these, Christ alone, was a fundamental principle of the Reformation because it was the criterion by which Luther judged both the theology and piety of the late medieval church. The function of this criterion was to preserve the uniqueness of Christianity by preventing anyone or anything from usurping the role of Jesus as sole redeemer of the world. The most direct threat to this role came from the elevation of Mary to co-redemptrix, but the cult of saints in general was rejected owing to the practices associated with it: praying to the saints instead of to God, assigning special miracles and protective powers to patron saints like Ursula and Christopher, collecting relics and depositing them in local shrines, promising miracles and indulgences to believers who made pilgrimages to those shrines, adding altars to specific saints that attracted more devoted worshipers than the main altar where Mass was celebrated, endowing fraternities and their chapels in the name of saints and hiring priests to say special Masses for themselves and their relatives. The cult of saints was popular because it gave believers more direct, specific, and personal access to sacred power than an awesome and distant trinitarian God could provide. Hence 'Christ alone' was not always well received by laity, or even comprehended by them. Why should they give up the personal and material channels of divine aid for one less tangible? Nor did they, even when they became Protestant. Luther and other reformers offered them guardian angels in place of saints (albeit with fewer trappings and less power), and believers gladly accepted.

The same challenge faced Luther and other reformers when they taught the right kind of faith and good works. The nuances of 'faith alone' were more difficult for laypeople to grasp than 'Christ alone'. In the new Christianity, 'faith alone' meant that God accepted believers only because of their faith in Christ and not because a meritorious 'good deed' supplemented their faith and made it effective. Nevertheless, good works were expected from believers because beneficial deeds always followed genuine faith. In his preface to the Book of Romans in the German Bible, Luther wrote that faith was 'a living, busy, active, mighty thing' that was incessantly doing works without asking whether they should be done or not. 'It is impossible', he said, 'to separate works from faith, quite as impossible as to separate heat and light from fire'. Readers and listeners consequently received the following message: 'You are saved by faith alone and not by good works, but you should be doing good works nonetheless. They do not earn salvation but they are necessary for living as a Christian.' That was the first nuance: good works were necessary, but not necessary for salvation.

The second nuance involved the definition of good works. In medieval practice, good works were mainly meritorious religious activities like those Luther listed above. They were directed towards God because the doers thought they were earning salvation. For Luther, those were the wrong kind of 'self-chosen' good works; but there was a right kind, which he explained in a remarkable treatise (published in 1520) that offers a straightforward introduction to Luther's theology and rationale for reform. The right kind of good works consisted of keeping the Ten Commandments and the first of these was faith itself, which fulfilled the Commandment to have no gods other than the Lord. In his small catechism, Luther explained its fulfilment by faith as simply as possible: 'We are to fear, love, and trust God above all things.' The opposite of faith was idolatry: trust in other gods of any stripe – idols made with hands, other human beings, noble ideals, or material goods. As the first genuinely good work, faith was directed towards God, as was honouring the Lord's name and keeping the sabbath, but not because obeying the first three Commandments earned salvation. Instead, faith in God was the source of all the genuine good works that were directed outward towards the neighbour in obedience to the remaining Commandments. These good works were not religious activities but the dedication of one's public and private lives to charity, honesty, sympathy, encouragement, support, aid, and justice. The contrast between proper and improper works was summarized by Luther in the following manner:

> Any work that is not done exclusively to bring the body under control or serve the neighbour (as long as he or she does not request something contrary to God's will) is neither good nor Christian. As a result I have great fear that few, if any, clerical associations, monasteries, altars, and offices of the church are truly Christian in our day. This includes the special fasts and prayers on certain saints' days. To repeat, it is my fear that in all these things we seek only our own profit, believing that through these acts our sins are purged and salvation is attained.

Despite frequent warnings not to neglect the neighbour, many listeners must have thought: 'Good works are not meritorious, so there is no reason to do good of any kind.'

Luther, of course, and the preachers who tried to convince people otherwise did not intend for them to neglect either church or charity. Religious activities were not meritorious and most of them had been discredited, but to nurture faith Protestants needed the religious resources of sermons, hymns, sacraments, catechisms, prayers directed to God, and familiarity with scripture. Luther and his colleagues set out to provide them. Long sermons on the biblical text in place of short homilies became the centre of Protestant worship, including those Lutheran and Anglican churches which adopted revised versions of the historic liturgy. All Protestant traditions made use of Psalms and hymns to enrich their worship and to express their devotion. In the German town of Joachimsthal, according to Christopher Brown, 'the most telling aspect of the reformation's success...was the use of Lutheran hymns within the home'. Some hymns were catechetical devices. 'Salvation Unto Us Has Come' by the reformer Paul Speratus was a summary of Protestant teaching. In 1534, Katharina Schütz Zell conveyed the importance of music in the preface to her edition of a songbook used by the Bohemian Brethren: 'I ought much rather to call it a teaching, prayer, and praise book than a songbook, although the little word *song* is well and properly spoken, for the greatest praise of God is expressed in song.' For teaching people the new Christianity, Luther published in 1529 small and large catechisms that were eventually used for instruction in most evangelical parishes, even though Luther encouraged pastors to write their own. Luther's catechisms contained explanations of three traditional texts: the Ten Commandments, the Apostles' Creed, and the Lord's Prayer, but they also clarified the new configuration of sacraments introduced into Protestant churches.

In a 1520 treatise entitled *The Babylonian Captivity of the Church*, Luther argued that the seven sacraments of the late medieval church should be reduced to three: baptism, the Lord's Supper, and penance, the last of which he called confession and absolution. According to his definition, sacraments had to be commanded in scripture and attached to both a spiritual promise and a material element that were clearly audible and visible when the sacrament was administered. For Luther, only baptism and the Lord's Supper unequivocally fulfilled these requirements. Water was applied in baptism, and bread and wine were consumed in the Lord's Supper, but no physical element was involved in confession and absolution. Soon penance was no longer considered a sacrament – especially because it did no more than renew the lifelong promise of forgiveness and salvation bestowed at baptism. In the Middle Ages, penance had become the most important sacrament because baptism marked only the beginning of a Christian life. Once sin was committed after baptism, it had to be confessed, forgiven, and satisfied by a penance assigned by the priest. Luther retained public confession and forgiveness and did not reject private confession, but penance was abolished because it had supported a piety of merit: penitent sinners were not fully forgiven until they paid the debt of their sin with the assigned penance or by acquiring an indulgence that excused them from the penance. For Luther, absolution from sin, whether public or private, took complete effect immediately because that free forgiveness was guaranteed through baptism. The promise of forgiveness and salvation applied in baptism was valid forever and became the foundation of Christian life at whatever age a person was baptized. For that reason, Luther retained infant baptism and considered it the most important sacrament.

Luther rejected the medieval interpretation of the Lord's Supper as, to all intents and purposes, a repetition of the sacrifice for sin made by Jesus on the cross, and he abhorred the abuses, like the multiplication of Masses, which that interpretation made possible. As a holy offering by the priest to God, the Mass was easily considered a miraculous good work that could earn merits for laity who either watched the Mass being performed or who paid priests to say regular posthumous Masses for themselves and their loved ones. Some people thought the more Masses they attended on a certain day, the more merit they would accrue; others were told they would not age during the time they spent at Mass.

For Luther, the Lord's Supper (also called Mass, Eucharist, Holy Communion) was not sacrificial but sacramental, that is, not an offering to God but God's gift to the recipients. It had been instituted by Jesus at the Last Supper and continually forgave sin by renewing the baptismal promise and strengthening faith. To emphasize its character as a gift, Luther and other Protestants made profound changes to the way it was celebrated. First, the Mass or Protestant communion service was celebrated in the vernacular instead of Latin. Second, the long prayer that accompanied the offering of the elements was replaced by the simple words of Jesus at the Last Supper (words of institution): 'This bread is my body given for you; this cup is the new covenant in my blood shed for you and for all people for the forgiveness of sins.' Third, in accord with these words and the pattern of the Last Supper, wine was not reserved for the priest but given after the bread to the laity who presented themselves. This reception of both elements (or both 'kinds') was the most moving alteration for some laypeople who took the cup, which they had never before touched, with trembling hands. The Mass was no longer a spectacle to be watched but a meal to be received by hungry souls with contrition, thanksgiving, and joy. Consequently, not everyone present at worship was expected to receive the sacrament, at least not in Lutheran churches. Confession and absolution, public or private, normally preceded communion, and only those who desired the sacrament were to partake of the meal. Reception of the sacrament was not an obligation, as it had been since the Fourth Lateran Council (1215), but a gift that should assuage consciences, not burden them. Nor was the sacrament a formality. 'If people were to become Christians merely because they received [both bread and wine]', wrote Luther, 'then nothing would be easier than to be a

Christian; even a sow could be a Christian.' Eating and drinking were not enough; recipients should listen carefully to the promise of forgiveness and believe it with a grateful heart.

Appearing in 1523, the *Order of Mass and Communion* was Luther's first revision of the Mass and a shift of strategy. Until that point, he had used only books and sermons to call people away from their 'ungodly opinions' about worship. The new structure, however, was designed not only to move hearts with words but 'also to apply the hands' and to produce tangible results. In 1526, he published yet another order for Mass, this time completely in German, and he prepared new liturgies for baptism, marriage, and other occasions. He also translated and composed more than 35 hymns, of which the best known has been 'A Mighty Fortress Is Our God'.

The earliest extant version of 'A Mighty Fortress' (*Ein' feste Burg*) appeared in print in 1531, but it may have been written as early as 1528. It was based on Psalm 46, and sundry occasions have been suggested for its composition: the Turkish threat, construction of new fortifications around Wittenberg, a regional epidemic, the death of his infant daughter Elisabeth, or the publication of a new hymnal in 1529. By 1900, over 80 translations in 53 tongues were available, and today it can be sung in 200 languages. Although sometimes attributed to him, the Christmas hymn 'Away in a Manger' appeared first in 19th-century America.

Luther refused, however, to make his orders for worship binding. Although correct external practices such as receiving both elements were important, the use of them was free, and they were always secondary to faith and love.

I have taught in such a way that my teaching would lead first and foremost to a knowledge of Christ, that is, to pure and proper faith and genuine love, and thereby to freedom in all matters of external conduct such as eating, drinking, clothes, praying, fasting, monasteries, sacrament, and whatever it may be. Such freedom is used in a salutary way only by those who have faith and love, that is, those who are real Christians. On such people we can and should impose no human law – nor permit anyone else to do so – which would bind their conscience.

Luther's vision for a new Christianity was utopian, and the controversies it ignited reminded him of that fact every day. He was attacked not only by his Roman opponents but also by former colleagues and others who thought his proposals for change went either too far or not far enough. Most Protestants agreed in principle that the Mass had to be reformed, but they could not agree on the nature of the Lord's Supper. Luther believed it was communion with the true body and blood of Christ, but other reformers, notably Karlstadt, Ulrich Zwingli, and John Calvin, thought the real presence of Christ's body and blood resembled the medieval doctrine of transubstantiation, according to which the substance of bread and wine was transformed into body and blood. Luther rejected the theory of transubstantiation, but he believed that Christ was truly present because Jesus had said the bread was his body and the cup was the new covenant in his blood. Zwingli, in particular, argued that Luther's view was too materialistic and would encourage popular superstitions like stealing the host (wafer or bread) and attributing to it miraculous powers. According to Karlstadt and Zwingli, Jesus intended for the bread and wine to represent his body and point believers to the cross where it had been sacrificed for their salvation. Luther insisted that communion not only recalled the sacrificial death of Christ, but that it actually conveyed the forgiveness of sin which his sacrifice had procured. The rift between Luther and Zwingli was never healed, and their followers gradually divided into Lutheran and Reformed churches that predominated in different parts of Europe.

Prayer was seldom a matter of dispute among Protestants, but their overhaul of late medieval modes of praying was rigorous and controversial. Using manuals and mnemonic devices like the rosary, late medieval people prayed earnestly and often to Mary and the saints; specific prayers might be rewarded with indulgences, as promised in devotional booklets like the *Little Garden of the Soul*. Published first in 1498 at Strasbourg, it was soon available in a German version that was adorned with fine illustrations and contained prayers to a host of holy figures for scores of personal and liturgical occasions. In the preface to his 1522 *Personal Prayer Book*, Luther sharply criticized the *Little Garden* and similar handbooks:

> Among the many and harmful books and doctrines which are misleading and deceiving Christians and give rise to countless false beliefs, I regard the personal prayer books as by no means the least objectionable. They drub into the minds of simple people a wretched counting up of sins and going to confession, plus un-Christian tomfoolery about prayers to God and his saints! Moreover, these books are puffed up with promises of indulgences and come out with decorations in red ink and pretty titles. These books need a basic and thoroughgoing reformation if not total extermination.

Claiming that he had insufficient time to undertake such a reform, Luther offered his own guide to prayer, insisting that the Lord's Prayer was sufficient at any time and that a persistent and heartfelt turning to God was more important than many words. Not known for brevity himself, Luther nevertheless carried that exhortation to an extreme that might offend pious ears. In a letter of condolence to an Austrian nobleman whose wife had died, Luther asked him to stop paying for all the vigils, Masses, and daily prayers being offered for his wife. Instead, he admonished:

> It is sufficient for your grace earnestly to pray once or twice for her. For God has promised that whatever you ask for, believe that you will receive it and you will certainly have it (Luke 11:9–10). In contrast, when we pray over and over again for the same thing, it is

a sign that we do not believe God and with our faithless prayer we only make him angrier. True, we should constantly pray, but always in faith and certain that we are being heard. Otherwise, the prayer is in vain.

During his later years, Luther expressed both contentment and disappointment with the new Christianity that was emerging from his efforts. A project as big as the Reformation was bound to result in both reactions. Although he insisted that believers justified by faith alone and diligent in loving remained sinners in need of forgiveness, Luther envisioned a Christianity filled with more saints than sinners. As later generations have proven, it was an ideal that could not be realized.

Chapter 6
The political reformation

On 25 September 1513, from a summit on the isthmus of Panama, the Spanish explorer Vasco Núñez de Balboa became the first known European explorer to lay eyes on the Pacific Ocean from the shore of the New World. Only 40 days earlier in Germany, Martin Luther delivered his first lecture on the Book of Psalms. From that day on, his career would rise in parallel with the expansion of the Spanish empire in the Americas. Between 1519 and 1521, when Luther's conflict with Rome was proceeding towards his excommunication and the censure at Worms, Hernán Cortés was pressing forward in Mexico to put an end to the Aztec empire and reporting the conquest to his monarch, Charles of Castile. After his election in 1519 as emperor of the Holy Roman Empire, Charles became Luther's monarch as well. Although the Reformation in Germany started as a religious protest, it was political from the beginning, and it would be Emperor Charles V, not Luther, who would determine its fate. Charles, a devoted adherent of Rome, had imposed the ban on Luther in 1521, but he still needed the support of Protestant towns and princes in order to protect Germany from the Turkish threat. Charles therefore sought to restore religious unity to his empire and, in so doing, allowed the Protestant movement to survive and eventually to flourish. Luther played a substantial role in this political drama, but after 1529 he was swept along in the current of events more often than he directed their flow.

Luther and his colleagues were involved in politics at every level – from local to imperial – because in Germany support for Luther's movement was authorized or denied by princes and city councils. In towns small and large, the following pattern of reform was typical. A priest who had been swayed by Luther started to preach the evangelical message of salvation by faith alone and to change the way Mass was celebrated. He might also condemn as unbiblical indulgences, praying to saints, fasting regulations, monastic vows, and clerical celibacy. If that priest attracted a sizeable following, he would be challenged by the Roman clergy in town and reported to the bishop of the diocese. The preacher would then appeal his case to the city council and ask them to approve his sermons and the alterations made to the Mass. In some cases, the council would hold hearings or stage debates between the evangelical preacher and a representative of the Roman clergy. Public demonstrations by supporters of both sides might be organized. At Göttingen in 1529, when Catholics were processing through town with the host, evangelical supporters blocked an intersection and sang a hymn version of Psalm 130 written six years earlier by Luther. When Catholics finally reached the church and sang the *Te Deum*, an ancient hymn of praise, the Protestants pressed in from the back and attempted to drown them out with another German hymn. If a city council decided in favour of the evangelical cause, as it did in Göttingen, then it would allow the preaching to continue and, in most cases, adopt a church order or constitution that made evangelical preaching and worship the religious norm of the community.

At Wittenberg during Luther's absence (April 1521–March 1522), the politics of reform were prickly and uncoordinated. The initiative was seized by his fellow Augustinian, Gabriel Zwilling, and his university colleagues, Andrew Karlstadt and Philip Melanchthon. Without waiting for approval from the elector or the town council, Karlstadt spoke out against clerical celibacy and monastic vows. Moreover, although he was a priest and archdeacon of the All Saints' clerical chapter, in January 1522 at the age of 35, Karlstadt married Anna von Mochau, a young woman less than half his age. In September 1521, Melanchthon, who was not ordained, and a few students received both bread and wine in the city church, and at Christmas Karlstadt offered both elements to the laity at a Mass in which he substituted German words of institution for the Latin canon or Eucharistic prayer. Unlike Melanchthon and Zwilling, however, Karlstadt maintained that laity who refused to drink the wine committed a sin – a position which Luther, writing from the Wartburg, strongly opposed. In the meantime, Zwilling was asking laypeople to withhold gifts from the Augustinian monastery so that friars would be forced to leave. In November 1521, thirteen of the brothers did quit the monastery, marry, and take jobs as labourers. In early December, a crowd of students and townspeople protested the saying of private Masses in the city church by grabbing missals and forcing priests away from the altars. The next day, thirteen students entered the Franciscan church and dismantled a wooden altar. Elector Frederick wanted the trespassers punished, but prominent burghers intervened with the city council, which now found itself caught between the elector and the citizenry.

About the same time, Luther, disguised as a knight called George, made a secret visit to Wittenberg and declared that he was pleased with everything he saw. Back at the Wartburg, however, Luther called for restraint in a short tract, the title of which said it all: *A Sincere Admonition by Martin Luther to All Christians to Guard against Insurrection and Rebellion.* After predicting that 'the pope and his anti-Christian regime' would be destroyed not by human violence but through God's wrath and the word of Christ, Luther disavowed the use of force and advised his followers to implement the following strategy:

> Get busy now: spread the holy gospel and help others spread it.
> Teach, speak, write, and preach that human laws are nothing. Urge
> people not to enter the priesthood, the monastery, or the convent

and hinder them from doing so; encourage those who have already entered to leave. Give no more money for [papal] bulls, candles, bells, [votive] tablets, and churches; rather tell them a Christian life consists of faith and love.

Neither Karstadt nor Zwilling took heed. After a meeting of Augustinians in Wittenberg concluded its deliberations, Zwilling ordered that the chapel be cleared of altars, crucifixes, images of saints, and altarware no longer needed for evangelical worship. Meanwhile, Karlstadt, who had earned degrees in civil and canon law, crafted a church order that incorporated all the changes made to that point by him and his colleagues. Elector Frederick was unwilling, however, to approve the new order because the imperial government had instructed him to oppose all innovations in Wittenberg. After Karlstadt's sermon against images ignited an iconoclastic riot in the town church, Melanchthon and the city council recalled Luther to Wittenberg to take charge of reform. He complied with their request even though Elector Frederick refused to give his permission and asked Luther to document that refusal. Luther absolved Frederick of responsibility but maintained that Wittenberg was his parish, 'my fold, entrusted to me by God', which he could not abandon. Furthermore, he feared God would punish the German nation with a 'real rebellion' because the people did not know how to use the gospel correctly.

Three years later, that fear was realized in the peasants' war or, more accurately, the revolution of 1525 because it was a full-scale uprising that cut across social and economic classes. The revolution had already begun in south Germany when Luther read the *Twelve Articles of the Peasants in Swabia*. Their stated purpose was to 'excuse in a Christian way the disobedience and even the rebellion of the peasants' by showing that their grievances and demands were supported by scripture. Luther responded to the articles in a pamphlet aptly named *Admonition to Peace*, because his greatest fear was still the potential of revolution, if unchecked, to cause anarchy or, as he phrased it, 'the permanent destruction of all Germany' by overthrowing both the word of God and civil authority. For that reason, he called both rulers and subjects to account. Princes and bishops were rebuked because they did nothing but 'cheat and rob the people' so that they could lead lives of 'luxury and extravagance'. Their wickedness and injustice, however, did not excuse disorder and rebellion by the commoners, because punishing wickedness, according to scripture, was the responsibility of legitimate government. Moreover, if the peasants claimed to be Christian, as they did, they must submit to the admonition of Christ to turn the other cheek: 'Christians do not fight for themselves with sword and musket, but with the cross and with suffering.' In the end, Luther declared that neither party had justice or Christian conduct on its side and recommended negotiation that required rulers to quit being oppressive tyrants and commoners to moderate their demands.

Instead of negotiation, the revolution expanded steadily northwards into Luther's vicinity. There, in May of 1525, the radical theologian Thomas Müntzer, who advocated destroying the godless prior to the thousand-year reign of Christ (Revelation 20:4–6), rallied his followers for the decisive battle at Frankenhausen. Against a combined princely force, however, they stood no chance and were cut to pieces; Müntzer, who was found hiding under a bed, was forced to sign a confession and then executed. Only weeks earlier, after observing the devastation wrought by roving bands of peasants, Luther had written that princes could slay them if need be to stop their marauding; after the slaughter, however, Luther was severely criticized and persuaded to publish a retraction. It turned out instead to be a defence of his argument that the commoners were rebels who deserved death because they were flouting government and destroying the social order. Luther also intensified his allegation that the princes were tyrants who could not get their fill of blood, but that part of his 'retraction' was forgotten and he was disparaged as a 'flatterer of the princes', a reputation that has stuck in spite of his insistence that he was simply instructing both commoners and rulers in their Christian duty.

6. Electors Frederick the Wise, John the Steadfast, and John Frederick of Saxony. Triptych by Lucas Cranach, c. 1535

Earlier in May of 1525, after tacitly allowing Luther to proceed with reform, Elector Frederick died in a demonstrably evangelical manner after receiving both bread and wine at his final communion. He was replaced by his brother John, a stout defender of the Reformation, who worked closely with the Wittenbergers to establish an evangelical church in Electoral Saxony. Seeing the parishes in disarray after the revolution and having no bishops on his side to perform their traditional duty, Luther asked Elector John to appoint a team of four visitors to examine the economic and religious state of the parishes. The inspection, or visitation as it was called, commenced in 1527, and Melanchthon and Luther prepared a set of doctrinal and practical instructions that became the first constitution of the reorganized evangelical parishes in Luther's region. The Wittenbergers were not, however, establishing a state-controlled church. The instructions distinguished clearly between church order and civil government:

> Every secular authority is to be obeyed not because it sets up a new service to God but because it makes for orderly life in peace and love. Therefore, it is to be obeyed in everything except when it commands what is contrary to the law of God, for example, if the

government orders us to disregard the gospel or some of its parts. In such cases we are to follow the rule of Acts 5:29: 'We must obey God rather than human authority.'

In practice, however, the consolidation and expansion of the German Reformation resulted from steadfast cooperation between evangelical rulers and theologians, because the threat of suppression, stemming from Emperor Charles and his Catholic advisers, was both political and religious. In 1526, seven Protestant princes formed the defensive league of Torgau, which, along with its successors, became the backbone of resisting imperial attempts to force evangelical estates (free cities and territories that had adopted the Reformation) back under papal authority. The estates gained some leeway when the first Diet of Speyer (1526) allowed each estate to manage religious affairs as it pleased until the matter was settled by a church council. In 1529, however, the Catholic states that dominated the second Diet of Speyer demanded that the agreement of 1526 be revoked and the edict of Worms from 1521 against Luther and his followers be enforced. The evangelical estates, then in the minority, protested this decree and formed the Protestant league of Speyer.

Another timely respite came from the advance of the Ottoman Turks into Central Europe, because Charles needed military and financial support from both Protestant and Catholic territories in order to defend the empire. After the Turks laid siege to Vienna in the autumn of 1529, Charles, with religious reunification in mind, asked both Catholics and Protestants to submit statements of their teachings and practices at a Diet set to meet the next year at Augsburg. Catholics ignored the request, but Protestant supporters of Luther, meeting in Saxony, prepared a set of articles that dealt with evangelical practices; Philip Melanchthon, who headed the Lutheran theologians attending the Diet, supplemented the practical matters with a list of evangelical teachings. At Augsburg in June of 1530, after the 28 articles had been discussed and revised by theologians, they were signed by seven German princes and representatives of two cities and presented to Charles as both a religious statement and a political declaration. Rejected by Catholic theologians and known thereafter as the Augsburg Confession, the articles gradually became a charter of the Protestant cities and territories that began to see themselves as Lutheran. Most Protestants left the Diet before an edict, issued in the name of Charles, renewed the outlaw status of Luther and gave the Protestants six months to suppress all the religious innovations in their domains.

Since he was certain of impunity only in Saxony, Martin Luther was not allowed to attend the Diet, but he did stay in touch with Melanchthon and other theologians through almost daily correspondence. Aware that the Diet was a watershed for the Reformation, Luther fretted about the outcome and urged his colleagues to stand firm. Once it was over, Luther wasted no time responding to the edict. In 1531, he published a *Warning to His Dear German People*, in which he sanctioned armed resistance if the edict against Protestants was enforced. The reformer had earlier counselled obedience to the emperor and supported a defensive war against the Turks, but after 1530 Luther reversed himself and argued that preservation of the gospel overrode civil obedience to a ruler who would obliterate it:

> If war breaks out – which God forbid – I will not criticize those who defend themselves against the murderers and bloodthirsty papists, nor let anyone else rebuke [the defenders] as seditious, but I will accept their action and let it pass as self-defence.

Near the end of the same treatise, Luther painted an exceedingly dark picture of what would happen if his followers did not resist the emperor:

> You will have to assist in the extermination and destruction of all [our accomplishments]. . . . You will have to burn all the German books, new testaments, psalters, prayer books, hymnals, and all the

good things we wrote.... You will have to keep everyone ignorant of the ten commandments, the Lord's prayer, and the creed, for this is the way it used to be. You will have to bar everyone from learning about baptism, the sacrament, faith, government, matrimony, or the gospel. You will have to keep anyone from knowing Christian liberty. You will have to prevent people from placing their trust in Christ and deriving their comfort from him. For all that was non-existent before; all of it is new.

Nothing like that happened until 1548 after Charles had finally defeated the Protestant leaders and captured Wittenberg. Instead, at the end of 1530, Elector John of Saxony and Landgrave Philip of Hesse convened a meeting of princes and urban officials at the town of Schmalkald to form a defensive alliance that was named after the town. In 1532, Emperor Charles agreed to a truce until the meeting of a general church council, and that stalemate, renewed in 1539, allowed the league to expand rapidly and become a formidable Protestant political and military bloc in the empire.

During the last 14 years of his life, Luther was the subject of a new elector in Saxony, John Frederick, who succeeded his father, Elector John, upon John's death in 1532. Far from trying to restrain Luther's sharp tongue in political matters, John Frederick encouraged the reformer to employ his well-known talent for polemics against the Catholic foes of the Schmalkaldic league. Luther was happy to oblige, especially since the main issue confronting the league was whether or not to attend the general council that was finally ordered by Pope Paul III to convene in 1537. Elector John Frederick did not think it wise to attend, and in early 1537 members of the league and other Protestants convened in Schmalkald to discuss the matter. For the meeting, Luther was asked to compose a theological testament that listed those topics which could or could not be negotiated at the upcoming council. In several tracts, he had already argued that a council called by the pope could never be a free and open forum, but in this testament, known as the Schmalkaldic Articles, he reasserted that the pope was the Antichrist and the papacy a human fiction of no use to the church: 'It would have been much better if such a head had not been raised up by the devil.' The prospect of a council led, however, to a significant historical and political treatise, *The Councils and the Church*, published in 1539. From church history, Luther attempted to demonstrate that councils had contradicted themselves and were therefore an unreliable basis on which to reform the church. Their primary function was to safeguard the ancient faith already recovered by the Reformation on the basis of scripture; as a consequence, a council convened by the pope could not possibly benefit the authentic Christianity that was being restored by the reformers.

Two additional conflicts involved Luther in awkward political controversy prior to his death. The first of these was caused by the bigamy of Landgrave Philip of Hesse, a Protestant stalwart since 1524, adept leader of the Schmalkaldic league, and a noted adulterer. In 1540, he married Margarete von der Saale without divorcing his wife, Christina of Saxony, with whom he had fathered ten children. At the insistence of Margarete, Philip sought the approval of theologians Martin Bucer, Luther, and Melanchthon by claiming bigamy was his only route to moral redemption and by threatening to support Emperor Charles if the reformers denied him their blessing. Reluctantly, Luther and Melanchthon gave their approval in the form of secret advice from the confessional, but the marriage was exposed and all involved were blamed for a crucial misstep. The bigamy alienated some of Philip's Protestant allies and destroyed his political credibility once it was revealed that he had promised the emperor to maintain neutrality in order to avoid prosecution under imperial law.

The second conflict resulted from a long-standing feud between the Catholic Duke Henry of Wolfenbüttel and the Protestant leaders Philip and John Frederick. Several incidents in 1538 exacerbated the conflict to the point that both sides resorted to printed broadsides that contained ridicule, coarse insults, and abusive language. Luther was asked to respond to one of these broadsides against John Frederick, whom Henry had caricatured as an obese and lying drunkard, heretic, apostate, and monster. The tract also accused Luther of calling his own prince 'Hanswurst', a clownish stock figure who wore a sausage around his neck. Luther denied the charge and turned the tables on Henry by labelling him 'Hanswurst' and denouncing him in the same coarse and abusive terms that Henry had used against the elector.

Luther's polemic *Against Hanswurst* did nothing to solve the dispute among the princes or to enhance Luther's reputation as a political satirist, but it did demonstrate the entwinement of politics and religion that coloured Luther's entire career and the initial settlement of the German Reformation in 1555. Its terms granted to princes and city councils that adhered to the Augsburg Confession the right, without interference from the emperor or any authorities, to keep the religion of their domains Lutheran and 'to enjoy their religious belief, liturgy, and ceremonies as well as other rights and privileges in peace'. The estates and princes who clung 'to the old religion' were guaranteed the same rights, and no estate was to 'try to persuade the subjects of other estates to abandon their religion'. A Germany that was religiously divided was not the outcome that Luther had envisioned when he declared that all he wanted was 'to arouse and set to thinking those who have the ability and inclination to help the German nation to be free and Christian again after the wretched, heathenish, and unchristian rule of the pope'. Nor was it part of the glorious universal monarchy that had been planned for Emperor Charles by his erstwhile grand chancellor, Mercurino de Gattinara. By 1556, Charles had had enough of politics and began to renounce his chequered domains piece by piece. The remains of the empire were turned over to his brother, Duke Ferdinand of Austria, and in 1557 Charles retired to a house in Castile that was next to the monastery of Yuste. For the 18 months left to him, Charles worked in his garden, satisfied his voracious appetite with fine food, played the flute, admired his collections, and went fishing.

Chapter 7
From monk to family man

The Reformation was triggered by disputes over religious practice. In England, it was the desire of Henry VIII for a male heir, while in Wittenberg the extravagant claims made for indulgences provoked Luther's Ninety-Five Theses. In Zurich, it was the flouting of fasting regulations, and in Strasbourg, it was the right of clergy to marry. The last of these disputes was just as important as the others, if not more so. In Western Europe, the requirement for secular priests (who were not monks) to remain unmarried (clerical celibacy) had been resolutely enforced only since the 12th century, although the oldest monastic orders had long since obliged men and women to take vows of celibacy. For reformers, the right of clergy to marry was not motivated solely by a desire for companionship, sex, and children. All three had been available to those priests who lived with concubines, and their numbers were large enough for bishops to allow the practice with only a slap on the wrist. The right to marry, argued reformers, would avert such hypocrisy and nothing in scripture prevented it. Marriage was a divinely instituted estate that God intended for everyone who desired it, and only very few, they thought, could remain single and abstain from sexual relations. In their 1522 petition to the Bishop of Constance for permission to marry, the Zurich reformer Ulrich Zwingli and ten of his colleagues confessed:

> We, then, having tried with little enough success, alas, to obey the law [of celibacy], have discovered that the gift has been denied to us, and we have meditated long within ourselves how we might remedy our ill-starred attempts at chastity.

According to the reformers, clerical marriage was a public demonstration of Christian freedom, a testimony to the central message underpinning their reforms. And demonstrate it they did. The shocking thing about the marriage of Andrew Karlstadt to Anna von Mochau, mentioned in the previous chapter, was not the fact that Karlstadt was more than twice her age but that the wedding took place at all. Their public engagement had occurred in the presence of colleagues Justus Jonas and Philip Melanchthon, who accompanied Karlstadt to the fiancée's home village; and the announcement he sent to Elector Frederick made explicit the connection between Christian freedom and marriage. Ulrich Zwingli and Anna Reinhart, a widow with three children to whom he was secretly betrothed for two years, celebrated in 1524 a public wedding in the Zurich minster. The betrothal, considered equivalent to marriage, had been kept secret for sensitive political and family reasons. The reformer Martin Bucer arrived in Strasbourg a married man after having left the Dominican order and wed Elizabeth Silbereisen, a former nun, in 1522. In 1524, he presided at the marriage of the earliest evangelical preacher in town, Matthew Zell, and Katharina Schütz, a reformer in her own right who published a bold defence of their marriage. By wedding a priest, she said, she was giving glory to God, supporting other women who did likewise, following what scripture explicitly allowed, and demonstrating a holy alternative to the scandalous conduct of priests who took concubines. The ceremony drew a huge crowd of curious and supportive citizens. In 1523, Luther's erstwhile Augustinian colleague, Wenzel Linck, had become the evangelical pastor in Altenburg, about 75 miles south of Wittenberg, and then announced he was about to marry. At Wittenberg, theological lectures were cancelled while Luther and many of his colleagues attended the wedding.

7. Katharina von Bora, by Lucas Cranach, 1528

In June of 1525, when Martin Luther and Katharina von Bora (1499–1552) married, they were late to the altar. Luther's close colleagues were already wed, except for Spalatin, who married six months later, and Amsdorf, who remained unmarried. Katharina had arrived in Wittenberg two years earlier and her story was well known.

She was born at her father's estate south of Leipzig but her parents, though of noble descent, were themselves no longer wealthy. After her mother's death, Katharina was sent to a Benedictine school, and five years later, at 10 years of age, she entered the Cistercian cloister of Marienthron near Grimma in the Saxon lands controlled by Duke George, who was resisting the Reformation. After Luther's ideas became known in Marienthron, several nuns wanted to leave the hostile environs and arrangements were made with the merchant Leonhard Koppe, who made regular deliveries to the convent, to facilitate their escape. During the night of Easter Sunday 1523, twelve of the nuns were whisked from Marienthron in Koppe's wagon and taken to Torgau in electoral Saxony. Three of the women presumably returned to their families, but the remaining nine were escorted ceremoniously to Wittenberg, where Katharina is thought to have lived in the large house of Lucas and Barbara Cranach. Not long thereafter, Katharina fell in love with Jerome Baumgärtner, a former student in Wittenberg whom she met when he visited the town again in 1523. After Baumgärtner returned to his prominent family in Nuremberg, he did not pursue the relationship and finally married a younger woman from a better family. Luther and Amsdorf then tried to bring Katharina together with Caspar Glatz, an older man who was the pastor in Orlamünde, but she refused to marry Glatz and told Amsdorf she would rather marry him or Luther if that were her only choice.

It turned out to be Luther, but no one is certain exactly how the agreement was reached. However, between the exchange of vows and the banquet two weeks later, Luther disclosed to Amsdorf the motives that impelled him to take this step:

> Indeed, the rumour is true that I was suddenly married to Katharina in order to forestall the unrestrained gossip that commonly swirls around me.... Nor did I want to pass up this fresh opportunity to comply with my father's wish for progeny. At the same time, I wanted to confirm what I have taught by practising it; for I find that many people are still timid despite such great light shed by the gospel. God has willed this thing and made it happen. I feel neither passionate love nor burning for my spouse, but I cherish her.

By 13 June 1525, when the wedding took place, Martin and Katharina had known each other for two years. Nonetheless, the simple ceremony, which took place in the Augustinian complex where Luther was living, caught most Wittenbergers by surprise. Pastor Bugenhagen of the town church presided and four more people witnessed the event: Justus Jonas (who later reported he could not help crying), Johann Apel (professor of canon law who had married a nun), and Lucas and Barbara Cranach. They also observed the ritual *Beilage*: Martin and Katharina lying together briefly on the marriage bed. Katharina's wedding band was probably the gold ring given to her by King Christian II of Denmark when he visited the Cranach house in 1523. The customary banquet occurred two weeks later because Luther invited his parents, friends, and others from out of town, including the aforementioned Linck and Leonhard Koppe, who had helped the nuns to escape. The university sent a silver loving cup for the occasion, and Elector John donated 100 gulden to the couple and allowed them to set up housekeeping at the monastery.

Luther's remark to Amsdorf that he did not passionately desire Katharina but cherished her did not mean that Luther entered upon a loveless marriage to make a point. He often expressed affection and appreciation for Katharina, and he had good reason to rely on her. Not only did she bear six children, but she was the energetic manager of a large household that included relatives, frequent guests, and students. She participated occasionally in the roundtable conversations recorded in *Table Talk* and wholeheartedly supported the work of reform. Katharina was also a savvy businesswoman who oversaw several properties, one of which was purchased in 1540 from her brother and was located at Zölsdorf near her birthplace south of Leipzig. It was a favourite destination where she spent weeks at the time. After the purchase, Martin teasingly addressed a letter 'to the wealthy lady at Zölsdorf, Mrs Doctor Catherine Luther, residing in the flesh at Wittenberg and living in the spirit at Zölsdorf, to my beloved'. As a gift for Katharina, in 1540, Martin arranged for the carving of a more elaborate entranceway to their home that is still known as the *Katharinenportal*.

When Martin died away from home in 1546, Katharina had just turned 47. Not long thereafter, she described to her sister-in-law Christina von Bora the depth of her grief: 'If I had owned a principality or an empire I would not have felt so badly, had I lost it, as I did when our Lord God took from me – and not only from me but from the whole world – this dear and worthy man.' Katharina lived almost seven more years, but they were hard times during which 'she wandered around in exile during the war that followed with orphaned children in extremely difficult circumstances and dangers'. During the Schmalkald War (1546–7), which the Protestants lost, she and the children fled Wittenberg twice, the second time to Braunschweig with Melanchthon and another colleague. Her appeal to the Danish king for permanent exile did not succeed, but he did provide a yearly income for her and the children after she reopened the monastery in Wittenberg as a boarding house. When the town was threatened by plague in 1552, Katharina fled towards Torgau, but she was injured when the horses bolted. Katharina was bedridden for three months before dying in December 1552 at the age of 53. She was buried in the church at Torgau and commemorated by an upright carved gravestone that depicts her in winter clothing and holding a Bible.

Martin and Katharina were survived by four of their six children. The first-born, Hans (1526–75), named after his grandfather, studied law at Wittenberg and in Königsberg with the support of Duke Albert of Prussia, an early proponent of reform. Hans returned to Wittenberg just a year before his mother died and afterwards served the courts of Weimar and Brandenburg as a jurist. During the Diet of Augsburg (1530), Luther sent a letter to Hans, who was turning four, encouraging the boy to study and pray diligently, and promising that, if he did, he would be allowed into a magical garden full of ponies with golden reins and silver saddles, luscious fruits, gold whistles and drums, and fine silver crossbows. Their second child, Elisabeth (1527–8), was born just as the plague was letting up in Wittenberg, but she died eight months later.

Less than a year after the death of Elisabeth, Luther reported to Amsdorf that Katharina had gone into labour and three hours later had given birth without difficulty to a 'healthy baby daughter'. This daughter was Magdalena Luther (1529–42), and Amsdorf was asked to be godfather to 'the said little heathen and to help her [enter] holy Christendom through the heavenly, precious sacrament of baptism'. During the Diet of Augsburg (1530), Luther received from his wife a picture of little Magdalena ('Lenchen'), who was only one year old, and thanked Katharina in return by offering suggestions for weaning that he had received from Argula von Grumbach, one of the few women whose writings in support of the Reformation are extant. In 1542, however, Magdalena died in her father's arms after a long illness. Luther's letters and *Table Talk* testify that the death of Magdalena was an extremely trying time for both parents and for her older brother Hans, who was summoned home to be with his sister at the end. Conveying the news of her death to Jonas, Luther struggled with his emotions:

> I believe the report has reached you that my dearest daughter
> Magdalena has been reborn into Christ's eternal kingdom. I and my

wife should joyfully give thanks for such a felicitous departure and blessed end by which Magdalena escaped the power of the flesh, the world, the Turk, and the devil; yet the force of our natural love is so great that we are unable to do this without crying and grieving in our hearts, or even without experiencing death ourselves. The features, the words, and the movements of the living and dying daughter remain deeply engraved in the heart; even the death of Christ... is unable to take all this away as it should. You, therefore, give thanks to God in our stead. For indeed God did a great work of grace to us when he glorified our flesh in this way. Magdalena had (as you know) a mild and lovely disposition and was loved by all.... God grant me and all my loved ones and all our friends such a death – or rather such a life.

Martin and Katharina were left with four living children: Hans and three others who were born after Magdalena: a son Martin (1531–65), another son Paul (1533–93), named after the apostle, and a daughter Margarethe (1534–70), who almost succumbed to measles and was only 18 when her mother died. Three years later, she married George von Kunheim, a nobleman and civil servant in East Prussia; autographs of five letters written by her father to her mother were preserved by Margarethe and deposited in Königsberg. Paul Luther studied medicine and became both a professor and personal physician to the dukes of Saxony. Martin studied theology and died in his thirties. All three sons accompanied Luther on his last journey, and they were in nearby Mansfeld when he died in Eisleben. They marched behind their mother and sister in the procession that followed the coffin from the city gate of Wittenberg to the castle church where Luther was buried.

Judged by the sources, the Luther home seemed as happy as it could be – for an abnormally large household headed by an ex-monk and ex-nun in a former cloister. Admiring commentators later portrayed it as the exemplary Protestant parsonage, but that was certainly not the case, whatever an exemplary parsonage was thought to be. Luther's correspondence reveals devoted and jovial relationships between parents and children and between Martin and Katharina themselves; moreover, the home was filled not only with people but with music. Luther loved music and called it an excellent divine gift that ranked just below theology. Visitors reported that Luther spent some evenings singing in harmony with his children, students, and guests. The cantor, Johann Walther, with whom Luther worked closely and who sang 'many hours' with the reformer, observed that his appetite for singing was insatiable.

If the Luther family and household were indeed happy most of the time, one reason may be that Martin and Katharina took marriage seriously even though they no longer considered it a sacrament. In opposition to the unmarried state required by monastic and priestly orders, Luther named marriage one of the genuine orders that God had established for humankind alongside government and the church. Luther called these spheres of society 'true Christian orders', not because he thought marriage was only for Christians, but because marriage, civil service, and public worship for all were superior to celibacy, withdrawal from public life, or seclusion within a monastic elite. Luther took umbrage at the medieval church's prohibition of marriage between Christians and non-Christians:

> Know therefore that marriage is an outward, bodily thing, like any other worldly undertaking. Just as I may eat, drink, sleep, walk, ride with, buy from, speak to, and deal with a heathen, Jew, Turk, or heretic, so I may marry and continue in wedlock with one. Pay no attention to those fools who forbid it. You will find plenty of Christians – and indeed the greater part of them – who are worse in their secret unbelief than any Jew, heathen, Turk, or heretic. A heathen is just as much a man or woman – God's good creation – as St. Peter, St. Paul, and St. Lucy, not to speak of a slack and spurious Christian.

Those 'fools' who forbade it would eventually include not only the Roman Church but also John Calvin.

Since the domain of marriage was for everyone, Luther rarely used the term 'Christian marriage' but instead advised believers how to live a godly life 'in the marital estate'. The issue was an urgent one for most reformers since they agreed that marriage in 16th-century Germany faced a crisis. One author declared the situation out of control with 'rampant divorce and desertion...where one partner abandons the other in emergencies just when they need each other the most'. In 1522, Luther wrote:

> The estate of marriage has universally fallen into awful disrepute. There are many pagan books which treat of nothing but the depravity of womankind and the unhappiness of the estate of marriage, such that some have thought that even if wisdom itself were a woman one should not marry.

In contrast, believers were to acknowledge marriage as a gift and institution of God; Christian spouses should regard each other with respect and take upon themselves the burdens and joys of bearing and raising children. Under certain conditions, divorce was permitted, but Christian spouses would forgive injury and bear with the wayward partner before taking steps to dissolve the marriage. Sexual pleasure was not forbidden, but Luther retained the Augustinian notion that intercourse was never without sin. Still, 'God excuses it by his grace because the estate of marriage is his work, and he preserves in and through the sin all that good which he has implanted and blessed in marriage.' That thought was graphically illustrated in a letter to George Spalatin, who wed a woman also named Katharina. After congratulating Spalatin and telling him that he hated to miss the celebration, Luther asked him to greet his wife most sweetly and continued:

> And do this as well: when you have embraced Katharina in bed with the sweetest kisses, think also to yourself: 'My Christ has given me this person, this very best creature of my God; to him be praise and glory.' I will predict the day on which you receive this letter, and that night in the same way I will love my Katharina in memory of you.

Luther's views on family and relationships have received mixed reviews. For example, Luther did not emphasize the integrity of the single life precisely because his agenda was to recapture the dignity of marriage from the exaltation of celibacy as a more perfect state. When it was not used 'to deny the aid and grace of Christ', however, Luther affirmed it was possible to live honourably as an unmarried person. The reformer's tendency to confine women to the domestic sphere and his sharp criticism of couples who did not want children reflected both the patriarchal culture of 16th-century Germany and the threat posed to every family by the early deaths of spouses and children. Nor, like most of his peers, did Luther approve of same-sex relations which in his day were scorned as 'the unspeakable sin', 'sodomy' or 'Italian marriages'. These terms appeared mainly in passages that blamed sexual misconduct by clergy on the requirement of clerical celibacy. On all these matters, Luther's opinions were formed by customary and prejudicial attitudes and by his way of reading the Bible, but some comments, like the following, were delivered with verve:

> The ancient doctors have rightly preached that marriage is praiseworthy because of children, loyalty, and love. But the physical benefit is also a precious thing and justly extolled as the chief virtue of marriage, namely, that spouses can rely upon each other and with confidence entrust everything they have on earth to each other, so that it is as safe with one's spouse as with oneself.

Chapter 8
Angels and demons

The deaths of two children in the Luther family was not unusual in 16th-century Europe. The climate was harsh, sanitation was poor, and epidemics were frequent. Although the century is placed by historians near the beginning of an early modern period, in terms of living conditions and cultural awareness it was still the late Middle Ages, and Martin Luther was a medieval man. The Americas had been discovered and for centuries Europeans had possessed some knowledge of Asia and North Africa, but Luther, like most of his contemporaries, still lived within the narrow confines of European Christendom. He did not conceive of his century as medieval or modern, nor did he divide Christianity into Catholic and Protestant denominations as they were later classified. For him, the Reformation was a watershed because it moved Western Christendom from a long period of captivity under papal rule to a new age that was free of that domination. From 1520 onwards, Luther was convinced that the Western church had to be liberated from 'the papacy at Rome', which had insisted that it alone was the church. The notion of church was now expanded by Luther to encompass every assembly of believers who lived in 'true faith, hope, and love'.

Alas, the grand vision of a universal church and a liberated Christendom excluded all non-believers and nominal Christians who did not agree with Luther's definition of 'true faith, hope, and love'. In his eyes, European Christendom was threatened within and without by 'papists' or 'Romanists' who were still loyal subjects of the pope, by non-Roman reform groups whom Luther called enthusiasts and sacramentarians (Anabaptists and the Swiss reformers), and by adherents of Judaism and Islam. Both Jews and Turks, as Luther referred to them, were already viewed as threats in the Middle Ages, but in the early 16th century the danger was felt more intensely as Jews were expelled from many countries and Turkish armies closed in on Central Europe. Luther regarded these threats as attempts by the devil to stifle reform and to bury the gospel before it could save Germany from the Day of Judgement that was surely near. The greater the opposition, in fact, the nearer the end had to be and the more resistance and prayer were required to save at least a few. Luther's belief in the devil was therefore more vehement than popular superstition because more was at stake: not only worldly good fortune but eternal salvation and the survival of Christendom.

Luther believed in angels, too, and spoke about them on 29 September when the festival of St Michael and All Angels was celebrated. Preaching on that day in 1530, he noted that the festival, like other saints' days, had formerly been celebrated in idolatrous ways that perpetrated lies and superstitions about Michael instead of teaching people to appreciate the guardian function of all the angels. Luther agreed with the common view that the devil, like Michael, was created an angel; the devil, however, became a tyrant who used his power to hurt people, unlike the archangel Michael, whose supernatural strength worked only to their advantage. People who thought the devil kept his distance and posed no personal threat could not appreciate the importance of angels. They should realize, warned Luther, that 'the devil is nearer to them than their skirt or their shirt, surrounding them more tightly than their own skin'. The duty of angels was to protect believers from the ever-present devil and the destruction he could wreak upon their homes, spouses, and children. Fortunately, every believer had been assigned a guardian angel according to the traditional proof text (Matthew 18:10), and all the angels wanted people to live in peace. Evangelical believers, however, did not worship angels or pray to them but only thanked and praised God that, because of angels, they saw more good than evil, the day was brighter than the night, more people lived than died, and their homes and communities were safe.

Despite the value of angels, Luther devoted most of his words to the devil, and that disparity was telling. Feeling constantly beset by the devil, he was more afflicted by that discomfort than consoled by angelic protection. As he saw the world, the devil had carved out his own kingdom and bound humanity with the chains of sin, so that injustice and bloodshed filled the world and nobody was able to claim innocence and escape judgement. Humanity was ruled by sin, death, and the devil – Luther's unholy triumvirate – and their rule would persist, in Luther's eyes, until the gospel weakened their hold and faith set people free. Even then, however, believers remained at risk according to Luther's explanation of the sixth petition of the Lord's Prayer ('And lead us not into temptation'):

> Although we have acquired forgiveness and a good conscience and have been wholly absolved, yet such is life that one stands today and falls tomorrow. Therefore, even though at present we are upright and stand before God with a good conscience, we must ask once again that he will not allow us to fall and collapse under attacks and temptations.

With Christian existence so fragile and constantly exposed to evil forces, Luther saw danger on all sides and transferred the malevolent influence of the devil to all those who opposed him and seemed to threaten his agenda. Besides, the world was nearing its end, and for Germany it was now or never to hold fast to the gospel, which was their only hope. Any threat to Luther's agenda was a refusal to allow God to save a remnant of believers. The struggles between Luther and his opponents thus dominated his life and took on apocalyptic significance. One year before his death, Luther looked back on his life and saw mainly a series of controversies. First came the indulgence affair, which he recounted in the preface to his Latin writings; this affair was followed, in Luther's memory, by the sacramentarían and Anabaptist affairs. Foe after foe seemed to rise up against him, the devil was at work in every one, and against them all Luther unleashed some of the harshest polemics recorded in the 16th century.

His later writings in particular contained callous and sometimes vulgar language against real and perceived opposition, most notably against the papacy and the Jews. By themselves, the titles of two late works illustrate their ability to capture unfavourable notice: *On the Jews and Their Lies* (1543), and *Against the Roman Papacy Instituted by the Devil* (1545). Even his close collaborator, Philip Melanchthon, whose eulogy at Luther's funeral was filled with praise for the reformer's virtues, felt it necessary to explain the invective. Responding to those who suggested that Luther was harsher than he needed to be, Melanchthon appealed to what Erasmus allegedly said: 'God gave this last age a harsh doctor on account of the magnitude of its ills.' Luther, however, was better with the axe than the scalpel and accurately described himself as a rough woodsman whose job it was to 'dig out stumps and trunks, hack away thorns and briar, fill in puddles and clear a path'. Recent attempts to account for Luther's insensitivity have been conspicuously complicated by events of the 20th century. After Pope John XXIII and the Second Vatican Council stimulated ecumenical good will, Luther's unbending condemnation of the papacy seemed uncalled for, although the doctrine and practices against which he raised objections remained for the most part unchanged. Despite his criticism of oppressive princes, popular movements for liberation and social justice made Luther's admonition to slay rebellious peasants sound like a perversion of the Christian message. Most damaging of all, the Holocaust and the use of Luther's anti-Jewish statements by the Nazi propaganda machine rendered his anti-Semitic outbursts nearly unmentionable.

Martin Luther, however, did not live in the 20th century but in the 16th, and to a large extent his excesses can be explained by the attitudes and conflicts that surrounded him. For example, the ambivalent relationship between Christians and Jews harkened back to the beginning of Christianity itself, and it steadily deteriorated with the rise of European Christendom. Popular hostility towards small Jewish communities had intensified in the late Middle Ages; outlandish charges such as desecrating the host and murdering Christian children were levelled against them, and they were expelled from most West European countries. Still, Jewish communities remained in Germany and contact between rabbis and Christian theologians persisted during the early Reformation. Protestant reformers were for the most part Humanists and shared the renewed interest in teaching and learning Greek and Hebrew. They also believed that a purified Christianity would appeal to Jewish communities, and consequently they entertained unrealistic hopes for the conversion of many Jews or, as Luther put it in 1523, the return of the Jewish people 'to their own true faith'. In his early lectures on the Psalms, Luther had argued that prominent Israelites, like Abraham and David who had believed God's promises, were models of Christian faith, and he praised the earliest Jewish-Christian communities as the 'faithful synagogue'. Luther's predecessors, however, had lumped unbelieving Jews together with heretics and evildoers, and Luther made a similar connection after he had given up on converting the Jewish people. In 1543, he wrote:

> Jews, Turks, papists, radicals abound everywhere; in their conceit all of them claim to be the church and God's people, regardless of the one true [Christian] faith . . . through which alone people become and remain God's children.

Within two decades, the Jewish people in Germany, for Protestant and Catholic reformers, underwent a transformation from potential converts to serious threats. Although it was nonsense, Luther shared that view and it led to the harsh rebukes contained in *Against the Jews and Their Lies*. The 'lies' were ancient beliefs, founded on their scripture, that Jews were the unique people of God with outstanding gifts like the covenant, the law, and the promised land. Their refusal to acknowledge Jesus as the messiah was degraded by Luther to blasphemy, which angered God and caused his blessing to be withheld from Germany. The concern that Jewish 'blasphemy' might undercut the work of reform may explain why reformers like Urbanus Rhegius and Martin Luther defended at length a Christian interpretation of messianic passages from Hebrew scripture. Rhegius constructed a protracted dialogue with his wife, Anna, claiming to make explicit what Jesus did on the first Easter when, 'beginning with Moses and all the prophets', he explained to the disciples on the road to Emmaus 'in all the scriptures the things concerning himself' (Luke 24:27). Luther devoted 85% of *On the Jews and Their Lies* to arguments that Jesus was the messiah prophesied in the Old Testament and 15% to the notorious recommendations that are usually cited: set fire to their synagogues and schools, raze their homes, confiscate the Talmud and other sacred books, forbid their rabbis to teach, and deny them both safe conduct on public roads and any occupations except farming and weaving. Several of these recommendations were also made by the Protestant Martin Bucer and the Catholic John Eck. To devote that much energy – within an overwhelmingly Christian society – to proving that Jesus was the messiah and to suppressing a small Jewish presence indicates how fragile Christendom must have seemed to its leaders.

It is not historically accurate, however, to draw a direct line from Martin Luther to the Holocaust as William Shirer appeared to do in his *Rise and Fall of the Third Reich*. It is true that many German Christians remained silent as the Nazi regime murdered six million Jews (and others), and Nazi propagandists did make use of Luther's writings. It is also true, however, that other German Christians (Catholic, Reformed, and Lutheran), especially those in the Confessing Church, spoke out against the atrocities and some of them, like Dietrich Bonhoeffer, were killed, imprisoned, or exiled for that protest. German Christians who condoned the murders did not do so primarily because of what Luther said. According to Johannes Wallmann, who traced the awareness of Luther's anti-Jewish writings in Germany:

> the misuse of Luther's writings...for the purpose of racial anti-Semitism originated after World War I not in Lutheran theology, but against Lutheran theology in the 'völkische Bewegung' [nationalistic pure-German movement]. That movement was based on a nineteenth-century romanticized notion of German ethnic and cultural superiority that supported the Nazi racist and pagan fantasy of a Third Reich.

Luther's critique of Islam was more nuanced than his treatment of Judaism, even though armies of the Ottoman Turks presented a genuine threat to Central Europeans and not an imaginary one like Judaism. Moreover, pamphleteers exaggerated the threat by casting the political conflict as a war between Christendom and Islam or between Christ and the Antichrist. Most of what Luther knew about Islam was derived from medieval writers, but he and Melanchthon both wrote prefaces for a revised Latin translation of the Qur'an published at Basel in 1542. Luther's other writings discussed a proper Christian response to the Turkish threat and offered comparisons of Islam with Christianity. Little, if any, of Luther's material was original, but it took on new relevance in light of the Ottoman threat and the Christianizing agenda of the Reformation.

Luther viewed Islam as a syncretistic religion composed of pagan, Jewish, and Christian beliefs, but it had 'no redeemer, no forgiveness of sins, no grace, no Holy Ghost'. Better then for Christians to be dead, he maintained, than to live under a government where their faith could not be confessed in full. Luther obviously had no place for Islam in a re-Christianized

Europe, but he did not advocate a crusade against the Turks. If the emperor, claimed Luther wryly, set about to destroy unbelievers and non-Christians, then:

> he would have to begin with the pope, bishops, and clergy and perhaps not spare us or himself; for there is enough horrible idolatry in his own empire to make it unnecessary to fight the Turks for this reason. There are entirely too many Turks, Jews, heathen, and non-Christians among us with openly false doctrine and with offensive, shameful lives.

Like Judaism, Islam also fit Luther's schematic criteria for a 'works-righteous' religion, whose adherents had to earn salvation through meritorious deeds. Nevertheless, he was impressed by hearsay evidence of Turkish piety and surmised that it would put a Christian monk to shame. The ceremonies and self-discipline of the Turks, who were 'far superior to Christians in these matters', could teach the papists that the Christian religion had to be more than ritual and morality.

Luther was reluctant, however, to shower Islam with too much praise. It might, he feared, lead some Protestants to deny Christ and follow Muhammad. Defections of Christians to Islam were not a serious threat, but the Muslim respect for ritual served the Reformation agenda well in two ways. It provided a foil for criticizing medieval religion, and it reminded Luther's readers that the essence of Christianity was not ritual but the way of faith and love. Luther also shared some of the unrealistic optimism held by other reformers for the conversion of Muslims. For example, if Christians were taken captive by Turkish forces, he speculated that the faithfulness, diligence, and patience of the captives might so impress their captors that some Muslims would convert. His 1541 appeal for prayer against the Turks urged that children be taught the catechism so that, in case they were taken captive during an invasion, they might 'at least take something of the Christian faith with them'. He did not, however, go so far as the

Zurich scholar Theodor Bibliander, who initiated publication of the revised Latin Qur'an. According to Bibliander, God desired to save all peoples, including Muslims, the gospel would soon appear in Arabic, and he was willing to travel as a missionary to the lands of Islam.

'Luther's boldness was incredible ... [He] was the first writer able to castigate abuse at its source, and perhaps the last.' The biographer H. G. Haile tempered this admiration for Luther's outspokenness by suggesting that the invective and scatological language of his later years were prompted partly by his antipathy to legalism and partly by the sorrow, regrets, and disappointment of an old warrior. Various maladies – uraemia, coronary disease, depression – have also been proposed as explanations for the unbecoming behaviour of the older Luther. All of the above may have played a part, but Luther's disregard for the usual social and literary restraints suggests other dynamics at work. As an excommunicated imperial outlaw, Luther had achieved his leadership of the evangelical movement at sizeable personal cost that bestowed on him a powerful sense of entitlement, which could be destructive and led him to disparage and dismiss opponents like Karlstadt, Thomas Müntzer, and Zwingli. They, complained Luther, enjoyed the fruits of his struggle without having risked anything for the victory. When the Turks threatened again in 1541, Luther blamed ungrateful Germans because they had not heeded God's word but instead had fallen into sects and heresies, which were saying aloud things they would never have whispered when the pope was supreme. The subtext was clear: instead of rejecting what Luther taught, his opponents owed him thanks for freeing them from the pope and should let him be the authority. At one point, Luther even had second thoughts about it all:

> If I had to initiate the gospel [movement] now, I would do it differently. I would leave most people under the papacy and try unnoticed to bring succour only to those with desperate and anxious consciences.

As a sign of hope and reconciliation, churches throughout the world were asked to sponsor trees in a special Luther garden in Wittenberg to mark the 500th anniversary of the Reformation in 2017. The Luther garden is being planned around a landscaped adaptation of the reformer's seal. Luther is widely thought to have said: 'If I knew the world was to end tomorrow, I would still plant an apple tree today.' So far, however, this statement has not been found in his writings. Scholars believe it originated in the German Confessing Church, which used it to inspire hope and perseverance during its opposition to the Nazi dictatorship.

Toward the end, Luther also complained of greedy nobility, thieving workers, devious lawyers, and usurious bankers, before concluding:

> Germany is ripe and bursting with sin against God and is even going so far as to justify itself defiantly before God. That unfortunately, makes me too much of a true prophet. For I had often said that if we did not bring punishment upon ourselves, the Turks would do so for us.

It could be even worse. For persecuting the word [of God] that called them to repentance, Luther warned:

> It would be no wonder if God let loose over Germany not only the Turks but also the devils themselves, or if he would long since have swept it away with a deluge.

Less than two years before he died, however, when he was worn out, he wrote to Linck calmly and optimistically about the outcome of the Reformation:

> For myself I desire a good hour of passing on to God. I am content, I am tired, and nothing more is in me. Yet see to it that you pray

earnestly for me that the Lord takes my soul in peace. I do not leave our congregations in poor shape; they flourish in pure and sound teaching, and they grow day by day through [the work of] many excellent and sincere pastors.

Luther thought what he said was true, and it had some validity – not because he had changed the world, but in spite of the world remaining much the same. At the end of his life, he was less idealistic and wiser than when he envisioned the liberation of all Germany from papal tyranny. 'A preacher ought to know the world', he said,

> not the way I knew it as a monk, when I imagined the world was so fine and proper it would embrace the gospel as soon as people heard it. What happened, however, was the contrary.

Afterword

Martin Luther was a forceful personality who attracted both admirers and disparagers. Among the former was the Augsburg reformer Urbanus Rhegius, who stopped in 1530 to see Luther at the Coburg fortress. After the visit, Rhegius reported to a friend in south Germany:

> Nobody could hate Luther after they have met him. Books give some notion of his spirit, but if you could observe the man more closely, if you could hear him treat divine matters with his apostolic spirit, then you would say being in his presence is much better than hearing about him. Luther is too great to be judged by another scholar. He will certainly remain a theologian for the whole world. I am certain of it now that I know him better than before.

Rhegius would have enjoyed the 2003 film by Erich Till that portrayed Luther as a heroic rebel, genius, and liberator. He was, to some degree, all three, but in practice he preferred order over anarchy, faith over cleverness, and moderation over licence. Most attempts to make Luther an unblemished hero have foundered on the temptation to capture him with simplistic labels that were half-truths at best. Even his friends and colleagues had misgivings. According to a confidential letter written in 1548, Philip Melanchthon felt he had been forced to play second fiddle to his more dynamic and famous colleague.

The heroizing of Luther in words and images began soon after the publication of his earliest works at Basel in 1518. The preface to that edition, written by the reform-minded Humanist Wolfgang Capito, admonished theologians to abandon the scholastic methods of their predecessors and to recapture the teaching of Christ by following Luther's concentration on the gospels and Pauline letters. At the end of 1519, the Nuremberg Humanist and city official Lazarus Spengler published a defence of Luther that praised the consolation he was bringing to burdened consciences – specified by Luther at Worms as the main reason for his resistance to the papacy. Spengler had reportedly heard both clergy and laity thank God they had lived to hear Doctor Luther and his teaching. In 1521, Hans Baldung Grien, a south German student of Albrecht Dürer, created a woodcut for a written account of Luther's appearance at the Diet of Worms. It portrayed Luther as a divinely inspired saint with an open book and a dove over his head that is surrounded by a nimbus. In 1523, Hans Holbein the Younger produced a woodcut showing Luther as the German Hercules, who was assaulting Jacob von Hochstraten, a Dominican scholar who had written against him. Already defeated and lying on the ground were Aristotle and five medieval theologians. That same year, the *Meistersinger* of Nuremberg, Hans Sachs, wrote a long poem in honour of Luther, 'the Wittenberg nightingale who was being heard everywhere'.

Scholarly and popular acclaim for Luther continued throughout the Reformation and beyond. Between 1562 and 1565, Johannes Mathesius preached a series of sermons on Luther's life that turned into the first extensive biography of the reformer. Mathesius had studied in Wittenberg and avowed deep appreciation for his teachers; but, more a pastor at heart than a theologian, he concentrated on Luther's practical writings and the benefits they brought. If Luther had written nothing but his catechisms and table blessings, the world could not thank him enough. Mathesius was also convinced that God would forgive Luther's invective and scatological exclamations since the reformer was an instrument of divine wrath against the papacy. In 1577, the *Formula of Concord*

8. **Luther as the German Hercules, by Hans Holbein the Younger, 1523**

attempted to resolve contradictory claims to the legacy of Luther by making scripture, the ancient Christian creeds, and the Augsburg Confession (1530) the standards of Lutheran teaching. The Confession was said to summarize the truth of God's word that was 'brought to light out of the horrible darkness of the papacy' by 'that most outstanding man of God', Dr Luther. By the 17th century, the miraculous power of incombustibility was being attributed to Luther's image. In 1634, a German pastor claimed that a copper engraving of the reformer had survived a fire that destroyed his study. About 50 years later, a portrait of Luther survived a fire that damaged his birth house in Eisleben. The picture, which depicted Luther between the crucified Christ and a rendition of the reformer's seal, was allegedly still hanging in the Luther house in 1827.

Disparagers of Luther were also numerous. The earliest were Catholic theologians and Humanists who opposed the reformer soon after his case was opened in Rome. Between 1520 and 1525, around 60 writers produced over 200 books and pamphlets against the Reformation, and many of them were directed at Luther. Most of their authors were competent scholars like John Eck and Thomas Cajetan, who had debated Luther face to face. Both men remained opposed to the Reformation and wrote careful defences of Catholic teaching on the sacrifice of the Mass and the primacy of the pope. Since they wrote in Latin, as did most Catholic controversialists, their books had less popular influence than the German pamphlets written in support of Luther. A notorious opponent of Luther was the English King Henry VIII. In 1521, with substantial assistance from his later lord chancellor Thomas More, Henry published a defence of the seven sacraments; the king also supported the anti-Lutheran writings of More and John Fisher, bishop of Rochester, who singled out key teachings of Luther for lengthy rebuttal. In 1523, More published a scurrilous response to Luther, which More's pseudonym, William Ross, touted as a 'choice, learned, witty, and pious work' that 'admirably exposes and refutes the frantic calumnies with which that most foul buffoon, Luther, attacks the invincible king of England, Henry the eighth'.

The first Catholic biographer of Luther, Johann Cochlaeus, published his polemical *Commentary on the Acts and Writings of*

Martin Luther of Saxony in 1549. Cochlaeus had earlier criticized
Henry VIII for executing his Humanist friends More and Fisher;
but Cochlaeus was staunchly anti-Lutheran, especially after
debating Luther privately in Worms. In 1529, Cochlaeus published
a notorious tract against the *Seven-Headed Luther* that accused
the reformer of rampant inconsistency. The woodcut on the title
page identified Luther with the seven-headed dragon (Revelation
12:1–6), which appeared to a pregnant woman clothed with the
sun and threatened to devour her newborn. Luther's seven heads
portrayed him variously as a doctor; a monk; a Turk; 'Ecclesiastes',
or the preacher telling the mob what it wanted to hear; a fanatic
with hair standing on end and surrounded by hornets; a 'visitor',
in reference to the Saxon visitation that allegedly made Luther a
new pope; and finally, as the robber released by Pilate in place of
Christ, Barabbas by name, depicted as a German wild man with a
club. The number seven was apparently useful to polemicists.
Defending his view of Christ's presence in the Lord's Supper,
Luther enumerated seven 'spirits' who had disagreed with him,
mainly other Protestants who refused to accept Luther's
interpretation of the words Jesus used to institute the sacrament.
The Wittenberger rejected outright any fellowship with those
'spirits', who by and large had responded to Luther with restraint,
at least with more restraint than Cochlaeus and other Catholic
antagonists had shown.

Cochlaeus suggested that Luther once suffered a fit during Mass.
When Luther heard the gospel lesson (Mark 9:14–29) about
the boy with the deaf and dumb spirit cast out by Jesus, he
allegedly fell to the floor crying, 'it is not me, not me!' This legend
fuelled suspicion that Luther suffered from a mental disorder,
especially after the psychoanalyst Erik Erikson made it the subject
of a chapter in his book, *Young Man Luther* (1958). Owing to his
overuse of sources that are not creditable, most historians reject
Erikson's pathological interpretation of Luther.

The prediction by Rhegius that Luther would become a theologian for the world turned out to be an exaggeration. Like his vision, Luther's impact was limited mainly to Europe, but the Europe he left behind was quite different from the medieval Christendom into which he was born. Little of northern Europe remained under control of the pope as Protestant churches were adopted by rulers in Scandinavia, the Baltics, Germany, England, Scotland, Holland, and Switzerland. These churches altered the daily lives of people whether the laity liked it or not. Saints were taken away from them, and pilgrimages on which believers hoping for miracles had crossed the continent from Finland to Spain were also discouraged. The spectacle of the Latin Mass was turned into a preaching service that demanded more attention from Protestant ears than from their eyes. The laity sang vernacular hymns, and when sacraments were celebrated, they received with the bread also the wine that had been withheld for centuries. The new printing technology increased the rate of literacy; for the first time in history, large numbers of people could own Bibles, read them at home, and take them on journeys. In hiding or in the open, Roman Catholics continued to live in all countries, but Protestant Christianity strengthened the regional and national forces that the medieval papacy tried to keep in check. The Reformation was also a boon for Protestant civil authorities, who used it to tighten control over their subjects.

The larger legacy of Luther embraces more than 70 million Christians in 79 countries who call themselves Lutheran. This statistic is regularly updated by the Geneva office of the Lutheran World Federation to which the vast majority of those churches belong. Most of these Lutherans still live in the European homelands of the Reformation – Germany, Norway, Sweden, Finland, the Baltic countries – and the roots of most North American Lutherans reach back to immigrants from those countries. In the United States, from the colonial period to 1850, it was mostly Germans who settled in Pennsylvania, Ohio,

Virginia, the Carolinas, and eventually in the Midwest; after 1850, it was mostly Scandinavians who pushed into the upper Midwest and beyond. Lutherans participated in the missionary movements of the 19th and 20th centuries and faced the challenge of transplanting their churches from Europe and North America into cultures around the world. The number of Lutherans is now increasing faster in Africa than anywhere else in the world. Wherever they are, however, Lutherans confront a fundamental challenge that goes back to Luther and the Reformation: how closely to cooperate with other Christians. On the one hand, Luther's view of the church was ecumenical. The gospel belonged to all believers wherever they were; their baptism and faith made a church of every assembly of believers gathered for worship. On the other hand, Luther cut off fellowship with those Protestants who did not agree with his views, and some Lutheran churches have followed his example in order to preserve, as they see it, the purity of his teaching.

Although Luther the reformer is well known, the best-known person with that name is the American civil rights leader Martin Luther King Jr (1929–68). His birth certificate identified him as Michael King Jr, after his father, who had already added Luther to his name and identified himself as M. L. King or Michael Luther King. After the father, King Sr, returned in 1934 from a meeting of the World Baptist Alliance in Berlin, he began to call himself Martin Luther King. In 1957, the name of Michael King Jr, was altered to Martin Luther King Jr, although he had used the name earlier. In his *Letter from Birmingham Jail* (1963), King Jr defended himself against the charge of extremism by citing the examples of Jesus, Amos, Paul, John Bunyan, Abraham Lincoln, Thomas Jefferson, and the reformer: 'Was not Martin Luther an extremist – "Here I stand; I can do none other so help me God?" '

Luther's intellectual legacy is harder to pin down. His writings did not contain a systematic ordering of concepts, and he speculated very little about metaphysical questions like the existence of God, with which modern thinkers have wrestled. At times, however, his theology, his person, and his deeds have stimulated religious leaders to take a new look at themselves and their world. The Methodist movement resulted in part from the impact made on John Wesley by Luther's preface to the biblical Book of Romans. Wesley immediately felt 'his heart strangely warmed' and received assurance that Christ had taken away his sins. Other European thinkers who read Luther viewed him through the lens of their own intellectual and political commitments. His appeal to conscience at the Diet of Worms inspired Enlightenment philosophers to see in Luther a champion of individual freedom against religious dogmatism. For example, Johann Gottfried Herder called Luther a true Hercules, who returned to all peoples, even those who did not accept his doctrines, the use of reason in spiritual matters. Others, however, came to very negative conclusions. Friedrich Nietzsche blamed Luther for undoing what the Renaissance had nearly brought to pass: the abolition of Christianity. Friedrich Engels accused Luther of betraying the peasants by giving them the Bible, on which their claims to freedom were based, and then using the same Bible against them to sanction the authoritarian might that quelled their revolt.

In the 20th century, the historical Luther was rediscovered through the methods of modern scholarship. Using his earliest lectures that had been recovered, edited, and published, Karl Holl initiated a Luther renaissance that by century's close produced hundreds, if not thousands, of articles and books by religious and secular scholars. The common foundation of all these works was the intensive analysis of Luther's German and Latin writings that were becoming available in the Weimar edition and in vernacular versions. The theological issues on which Holl had focused – justification by faith, its effect on the conscience, and Luther's reformation discovery – dominated Luther scholarship for most of the century, especially among theologians in Europe and North America. Gradually, however, Luther scholarship adjusted to new developments in Reformation studies, and scholars from a variety of disciplines began to study Luther. Specialists in German language, art and music historians, philosophers, scholars specializing in political and religious history all began to examine the reformer's significance for their disciplines. Luther and the Reformation no longer dominate study of the late Renaissance or early modern Europe as they did in the heyday of university courses entitled 'Renaissance and Reformation'. Many historians now question the concept of one Reformation and prefer to speak of the 'reformations' of the 16th century.

In 1983, the 500th anniversary of Luther's birth strengthened public awareness of Luther in Europe and the United States where the Reformation had its greatest impact. Soon thereafter, the reunification of Germany in 1989 made it easier to visit Wittenberg and other sites associated with his life. The Lutherhalle in Wittenberg, located in the Augustinian complex that was the Luthers' residence, is not only a museum with regular exhibitions but also a vital hub of Luther research with its expert staff and its repository of Reformation pamphlets, books, images, and artefacts. In 2017, the 13th International Congress on Luther Research will meet in Wittenberg as part of the celebrations that mark the 500th anniversary of Martin Luther's Ninety-Five Theses and the beginning of the Reformation.

Other challenges have presented themselves to current Luther scholarship: the disappearance of Christendom, the interpenetration of cultures and the proximity of religions to one another, fundamentalism of all kinds, a different way of waging war, vocal agnosticism and atheism. Luther's writings can be mined for insights on these and other matters, but his legacy is tied first and foremost to the future of Christianity and of religion in general. On the surface, his writings are not helpful starting points for inter-religious dialogue. They were so coloured by the anti-Judaism of late medieval Europe, the Turkish threat, and unreliable information that other facets of his thought could be more productive. For example, Luther insisted that religion was not mainly about personal morality but about faith and justice, not about making oneself good enough for salvation but about improving the lives of others in accord with God's original intention for humanity. In theology, Luther said, there was a 'new kind of doing' that was different from moral performance. Using religion to better oneself at the expense of others was idolatry, the sin of which he accused medieval Christendom. The opposite of idolatry was faith and love: trusting in God and serving the neighbour. Luther obviously filled this template of true religion with Christian content since his agenda was to recover for Germany an authentic Christendom. It could, however, be a useful criterion for determining the value of religion for any society, especially in the ongoing debate over whether religion does more harm than good. The best parts of Luther's legacy may be his eschewal of fundamentalism and his insistence that religion was not a way to appease the gods and gain their favour – but a constant reminder to place the world and its needs above selfish desires.

References and further reading

The best guide to the individual writings and main editions of Luther's works in Latin, German, French, and English is the *Hilfsbuch zum Lutherstudium* edited by Kurt Aland (4th edn., 1996). The pamphlets and books that were printed prior to Luther's death in 1546 have been catalogued in two volumes by Josef Benzing and Helmut Claus in *Lutherbibliographie* (1989/1994). The Kessler Reformation collection in the Pitts Library at Emory University contains over 3,500 Bibles, books, and pamphlets printed no later than 1570 and attributed to Martin Luther, his friends, and opponents. Available online from the same collection is a digital collection of woodcuts from Reformation pamphlets (<http://www.pitts.emory.edu/dia/woodcuts.htm>). The most thorough ongoing bibliography of new editions, translations, and writings about Luther appears annually in *Lutherjahrbuch* (Göttingen, 1919ff.). The recent *Luther Handbuch* edited by Albrecht Beutel (Tübingen, 2006) has brief surveys of newer editions, aids, and histories of Luther research, plus essays on Luther's life and work and a manageable bibliography and index. The most versatile visual resource is the CD-ROM produced by Helmar Junghans, *Martin Luther: Exploring His Life and Times, 1483–1546*. Available in German (1998) and English (1999), it contains everything historical, theological, biographical, and textual relating to Luther and his world in formats that include illustrated explanations, chronologies, images of people and texts, listings, plus an animated story of Luther's life for children of all ages.

For most of his career, Martin Luther exhibited an astounding capacity for work. The words put on paper by him or recorded by listeners fill over 100 large volumes in the only critical edition that aspires to completeness. The first volume of this Weimar edition appeared in 1883 during the 400th anniversary of Luther's birth; after 126 years, the last volume appeared in 2009, but documents are still being found that contain new material or require revision of works edited decades ago. The Weimar edition has four sections. The first 60 volumes contain Luther's lectures, sermons, postils, disputations, polemical writings, pedagogical and political essays, prefaces composed for a variety of publications, hymns, liturgies, and consolatory pieces dedicated to victims of religious persecution. Five volumes each of indexes to the Latin and German writings plus other index volumes complete section one (abbreviated WA). The second section (WABr) contains Luther's correspondence. Over 3,700 documents, of which 2,650 items were written by Luther himself, are edited in the first 13 volumes. The remaining volumes in this section contain excellent indexes. The third section (WADB) assembles documents by Luther and his colleagues that arose in connection with their translation of the Bible. In addition to German texts of biblical books, these 12 volumes include a revision of the Latin Vulgate and a record of how the German translation was revised. The fourth and final section (WATR) presents in six volumes a collation of earlier editions of Luther's *Table Talk*. Owing to its careful preparation and helpful indexes, the *Table Talk* has gradually gained credibility as a reliable source of Luther's life and thought when it is judiciously interpreted. The Weimar edition is readable and searchable online from Chadwyck at <http://www.luther. chadwyck.co.uk>. In addition, the publisher (Hermann Böhlaus Nachfolger Weimar) has made available at a reasonable price easily readable reprints of all four sections of the Weimar edition.

Hundreds of books and essays about Luther are available, but once an introduction or biography has provided sufficient background, Luther is best consulted directly about himself. Reader-friendly editions and translations are available in many languages, including English, German, French, Spanish, Italian, Hungarian, Chinese, Finnish, Norwegian, Swedish, Portuguese, and Korean. For English readers, the American edition of *Luther's Works* (LW) in 55 volumes (1955–86) published by Fortress Press and Concordia Publishing House is being expanded by Concordia; and Fortress Press is issuing separately new translations of key works in a series named *Luther Study Edition*. *Luther's Works* is also available on CD-ROM. A good place to start is not the Ninety-Five Theses, but treatises from the 1520s like *Freedom of a Christian* and the *Treatise on Good Works*. They present the most lucid and accessible contrast of Luther's theology and proposals for reform with the medieval religion he wanted to change. Then sample Luther's correspondence, for example in the excellent edition by Gottfried Krodel in volumes 48–50 of the American edition, and this complicated man and his world with all its peaks and valleys will come alive. The *Martin Luther Studienausgabe* (StA: Berlin and Leipzig 1979–) contains recent scholarly introductions to selected Luther writings with 16th-century orthography and a glossary of early new High German. For more assistance with reading Luther in Latin and German, consult the following: Birgit Stolt, 'Germanistische Hilfsmittel zum Lutherstudium', *Lutherjahrbuch*, 46 (1979), 120–35; Johannes Schilling, 'Latinistische Hilfsmittel zum Lutherstudium', *Lutherjahrbuch*, 55 (1988), 83–101. Available also is a recent three-volume edition of selected Luther texts in Latin with German translation on facing pages (Leipzig, 2006–9).

Websites

Many websites on Luther and the Reformation contain inaccurate content, but the following offer helpful and reliable information. (All accessed 23 June 2010.)

<http://www.luther2017.de/> The official website of the Luther decade (2008–17) with news updates and information about the Reformation jubilee 2017 and pictures from Luther sites.

<http://www.ecumenical-institute.org/> The Institute for Ecumenical Research in Strasbourg offers seminars, conferences, dialogues, and publications to enhance relations between Lutherans and other churches.

<http://www.lutheranworld.org/> The Lutheran World Federation, which has the most up-to-date information about Lutheran ecumenism and churches around the world.

<http://www.martinluther.de/> Website of the Lutherhalle in Wittenberg, one of four Luther museums that comprise the Stiftung Luthergedenkstätten in Sachsen Anhalt, a foundation that provides information about museums, research, educational offerings, and databases for learning about the Reformation and visiting the Luther memorial sites.

<http://www.luther-gesellschaft.com/> The Luther-Gesellschaft is a scholarly society that holds conferences and promotes research and publications on Martin Luther and the Reformation, including the journal *Luther*, published three times a year, and the annual *Lutherjahrbuch*.

<http://www.lutheranquarterly.com/> The *Lutheran Quarterly Journal* and *Lutheran Quarterly Books* feature essays, book reviews, and monographs on Luther and Lutheranism.

The Society for Reformation Research sponsors conference sessions, awards, and the *Archive for Reformation History*, which is published jointly with its European counterpart.

Books and articles

Resources consulted for this book and for additional information on Martin Luther's life, thought, and writings:

Matthieu Arnold, *La Correspondance de Luther* (Mainz, 1996).

David V. N. Bagchi, *Luther's Earliest Opponents* (Minneapolis, 1991).

Albrecht Beutel, 'Das Lutherbild Friedrich Nietzsches', *Lutherjahrbuch*, 72 (2005), 119–46.

Albrecht Beutel (ed.), *Luther Handbuch* (Tübingen, 2005).

Biblia Germanica 1545, facsimile edn. (Stuttgart, 1967).

Peter Blickle, *The Revolution of 1525* (Baltimore and London, 1991; German, 1977).

Heinrich Bornkamm, *Martin Luther in der Mitte seines Lebens* (Göttingen, 1979).

Gerhard Bott and Bernd Moeller, *Martin Luther und die Reformation in Deutschland*, Exhibition in the German National Museum, Nuremberg, 1983 (Frankfurt, 1983).

Martin Brecht, *Martin Luther*, 3 vols (Stuttgart, 1981–7; English tr., 1985–93).

Christopher B. Brown, *Singing the Gospel* (Cambridge, MA, 2005).

Georg Buchwald, *Luther-Kalendarium* (Leipzig, 1929).

Clayborne Carson et al. (eds.), *Papers of Martin Luther King, Jr*, Vol. 1: *Called to Serve*, January 1929–June 1951 (Berkeley, CA, 1992).

Irene Dingel, Günther Wartenberg, and Michael Beyer (eds.), *Die Theologische Fakultät Wittenberg 1502–1602* (Leipzig, 2002).

Angelika Dörfler-Dierken, 'Luther und die heilige Anna', *Lutherjahrbuch*, 64 (1997), 19–46.

Mark U. Edwards, Jr, *Luther and the False Brethren* (Stanford, 1975).

Mark U. Edwards, Jr, *Luther's Last Battles* (Ithaca and London, 1983).

Tibor Fabiny, *Martin Luther's Last Will and Testament* (Dublin and Budapest, 1982).

Leif Grane, *Martinus Noster: Luther in the German Reform Movement 1518–1521* (Mainz, 1994).

H. G. Haile, *Luther: An Experiment in Biography* (Garden City, NY, 1980).

John M. Headley, *Luther's View of Church History* (New Haven, 1963).

Scott H. Hendrix, *Luther and the Papacy* (Philadelphia, 1981).

Scott H. Hendrix, *Luther: Pillars of Theology* (New York and Nashville, 2009).

Scott H. Hendrix, 'Luther on Marriage', in *Harvesting Martin Luther's Reflections on Theology, Ethics, and the Church*, ed. Timothy Wengert (Grand Rapids, MI, 2004), 169–84.

Scott H. Hendrix, 'Martin Luther, Reformer', in *Cambridge History of Christianity*, vol. 6: *Reform and Expansion 1500–1600*, ed. R. Po-chia Hsia (Cambridge, UK, 2007), 3–19.

Hans J. Hillerbrand (ed.), *The Reformation: A Narrative History Related by Contemporary Observers and Participants* (Grand Rapids, MI, 1982).

Hans J. Hillerbrand, *The Division of Christendom* (Louisville and London, 2007).

Helmar Junghans, *Der junge Luther und die Humanisten* (Weimar, 1984).

Helmar Junghans, *Martin Luther und Wittenberg* (Munich and Berlin, 1996).

Helmar Junghans, *Spätmittelalter, Luther's Reformation, Kirche in Sachsen*, ed. Michael Beyer and Günther Wartenberg (Leipzig, 2001).

Helmar Junghans (ed.), *Leben und Werk Martin Luthers von 1526 bis 1546*, 2 vols (Göttingen, 1983).

Susan Karant-Nunn and Merry Wiesner-Hanks (ed. and tr.), *Luther on Women: A Sourcebook* (Cambridge, UK, 2003).

Erika Kohler, *Martin Luther und der Festbrauch* (Cologne and Graz, 1959).

Robert Kolb, *Martin Luther as Prophet, Teacher, and Hero* (Grand Rapids, MI, 1999).

Robert Kolb, *Martin Luther as Confessor of the Faith* (Oxford, 2009).

Robert Kolb and Timothy Wengert (eds.), *The Book of Concord* (Minneapolis, 2000).

Ulrich Köpf, 'Kurze Geschichte der Weimarer Lutherausgabe', in *D. Martin Luthers Werke: Sonderedition der kritischen Weimarer Ausgabe* (Weimar, 2000), 1–24.

Beth Kreitzer, *Reforming Mary* (Oxford, 2004).

Robin Leaver, *Luther's Liturgical Music* (Grand Rapids, MI, 2006).

Hartmut Lehmann, 'Anmerkungen zur Entmythologisierung der Luthermythen 1883–1983', *Archiv für Kulturgeschchte*, 68 (1986), 457–77.

Volker Leppin, *Martin Luther* (Darmstadt, 2006).

Elsie Anne McKee, *Katharina Schütz Zell*, 2 vols (Leiden, 1999).

Harald Meller (ed.), *Fundsache Luther: Archäologen auf den Spuren des Reformators* (Stuttgart, 2008).

Bernd Moeller, *Luther-Rezeption*, ed. Johannes Schilling (Göttingen, 2001).

Johann Baptist Müller (ed.), *Die Deutschen und Luther* (Stuttgart, 1983).

Nikolaus Müller (ed.), *Die Wittenberger Bewegung*, 2nd edn. (Leipzig, 1911).

Heiko A. Oberman, *Luther: Man between God and the Devil* (New Haven, CT, 1989; German, 1982).

Joachim Ott and Martin Treu (eds.), *Luthers Thesenanschlag – Faktum oder Fiktion* (Leipzig, 2008).

Jaroslav Pelikan (ed.), *Interpreters of Luther* (Philadelphia, 1968).

Volker Press and Dieter Stievermann (eds.), *Martin Luther: Probleme seiner Zeit* (Stuttgart, 1986).

Joachim Rogge (ed.), *1521–1971: Luther in Worms, Ein Quellenbuch* (Witten, 1971).

Otto Scheel (ed.), *Dokumente zur Luthers Entwicklung*, 2nd edn. (Tübingen, 1929).

Martin Schloemann, *Luthers Apfelbäumchen? Ein Kapitel deutscher Mentalitätsgeschichte seit dem Zweiten Weltkrieg* (Göttingen, 1994).

Klaus Scholder and Dieter Kleinmann (eds.), *Protestantische Profile* (Königstein, 1983).

Reinhard Schwarz, *Luther* (Göttingen, 1986).

R. W. Scribner, 'Luther Myth' and 'Incombustible Luther', in *Popular Culture and Popular Movements in Reformation Germany* (London, 1987), 301–53.

Ian Siggins, *Luther and His Mother* (Philadelphia, 1981).

Jeanette C. Smith, 'Katharina von Bora through Five Centuries: A Historiography', *Sixteenth Century Journal*, 30 (1999), 745–74.

David Steinmetz, *Luther and Staupitz* (Durham, NC, 1980).

David Steinmetz, *Luther in Context*, 2nd edn. (Grand Rapids, MI, 2002).

Kenneth Strand (ed.), *Luther's September Bible in Facsimile* (Ann Arbor, MI, 1972).

Martin Treu, *'Lieber Herr Käthe' – Katharina von Bora, die Lutherin*, Catalogue for the 1999 Exhibition in the Lutherhalle (Wittenberg, 1999).

Martin Treu, *Katharina von Bora*, 3rd edn. (Wittenberg, 1999).

Elizabeth Vandiver, Ralph Keen, and Thomas D. Frazel, *Luther's Lives: Two Contemporary Accounts of Martin Luther* (Manchester, 2002).

Johannes Wallmann, 'The Reception of Luther's Writings on the Jews from the Reformation to the End of the 19th Century', *Lutheran Quarterly*, 1 (1987), 72–97.

Wilhelm Weber, 'Das Lutherdenkmal in Worms', in *Der Reichstag zu Worms von 1521*, ed. Fritz Reuter (Worms, 1971), 490–510.

James M. Weiss, 'Erasmus at Luther's Funeral: Melanchthon's Commemorations of Luther in 1546', *Sixteenth Century Journal*, 16 (1985), 91–114.

Timothy Wengert (ed.), *The Pastoral Luther* (Grand Rapids, MI, 2009).

Jared Wicks, *Luther's Reform* (Mainz, 1992).

Ernst W. Zeeden, *Martin Luther und die Reformation im Urteil des deutschen Luthertums*, 2 vols (Freiburg, 1950, 1952).

Chronology

1521	Excommunication; Diet of Worms; declared imperial outlaw; taken secretly to the Wartburg fortress above Eisenach
1521–2	Seclusion at the Wartburg; unrest in Wittenberg and a secret visit; German New Testament, postils, *Monastic Vows* dedicated to father Hans
1522	Returns to Wittenberg and displaces Karlstadt; eight Invocavit sermons; *Little Prayer Book*; *Estate of Marriage*
1523	Katharina von Bora flees Marienthron and arrives in Wittenberg; *Temporal Authority*; former Augustinian superior Wenzel Linck marries
1524	First Wittenberg hymnal; appeals to city councils in Germany to establish Christian schools; stops wearing monastic garb in public
1525	Revolution of 1525; *Admonition to Peace* and *Against the Robbing and Murdering Hordes of Peasants*; Frederick the Wise dies; his brother John becomes elector; Martin and Katharina marry; *The Bound Will*
1526	*German Mass*; birth of son Hans; Lord's Supper controversy begins
1527	Epidemic in Wittenberg; birth of daughter Elisabeth
1528	Saxon visitation; Elisabeth dies; 'A Mighty Fortress Is Our God'
1529	Catechisms; Turks besiege Vienna; daughter Magdalena born; protest at the Diet at Speyer; with Zwingli at the Marburg colloquy
1530	Diet of Augsburg; Luther at the Coburg; father Hans dies; *Augsburg Confession*
1531	Lectures on Galatians; mother Margaret dies; son Martin born; Schmalkaldic league is formed
1532	John Frederick becomes elector; moratorium on enforcing the edicts of Worms and Augsburg allows Protestant expansion
1533	Son Paul born; academic disputations resumed at Wittenberg

1534	Complete German Bible published; daughter Margarete born
1535	Galatians lectures published; Luther becomes dean of the theological faculty and begins to lecture on Genesis
1536	South German theologians and Wittenbergers negotiate agreement on the Lord's Supper
1537	*Schmalkaldic Articles*; Schmalkaldic league meets; attack of kidney stones
1539–40	First volume of collected German writings published; *The Councils and the Churches*; bigamy of Philip of Hesse
1541	Revised edition of the German Bible; *Against Hanswurst*; *Admonition to Prayer against the Turks*
1542	Hymn 'Lord Keep Us Steadfast in Your Word'; daughter Magdalena dies; Luther's will leaves everything to Katharina
1543	*Against the Jews and Their Lies*
1545	First volume of collected Latin writings; *Against the Papacy Instituted by the Devil*; Council of Trent opens; concludes lectures on Genesis
1546	Luther dies on 18 February in Eisleben; burial in the castle church at Wittenberg
1547	Wittenberg seized by Emperor Charles V; John Frederick and Philip of Hesse are captured; Katharina Luther and children flee
1552	Katharina dies in Torgau; Protestant princes unite against Charles V
1555	Peace of Augsburg grants legitimacy to Lutheran cities and territories
1558	Emperor Charles V dies in Spain
1560	Philip Melanchthon dies in Wittenberg

Glossary and biography

Nicholas von Amsdorf (1483–1565): Wittenberg professor, priest, friend of Luther, who was present at the Leipzig debate and the Diet of Worms; after 1524, Lutheran pastor in Magdeburg and zealous defender of Luther's teaching.

Anabaptists: pejorative term for radical supporters of *Zwingli* in Zurich, who broke with him and the city's reformation in 1525 by adopting believers' baptism.

Apocrypha: sacred books mostly from late Judaism that early Christianity did not include in the Old Testament but were incorporated into the German Bible of 1534 because Luther considered them good and useful to read.

Augustine (354–430): influential North African bishop, saint, doctor of the church, and Luther's favourite theologian.

Augustinians (1256–): a mendicant (not strictly cloistered) religious order named after *Augustine* and joined by Luther in 1505.

Matthew Aurogallus (c. 1490–1543): Hebrew scholar from Bohemia and professor in Wittenberg, author of a Hebrew grammar, and crucial member of the team that translated the Old Testament into German.

Bernard of Clairvaux (1090–1153): Cistercian abbot, church politician, and mystical theologian often cited by Luther.

Theodor Bibliander (1506–64): linguist, professor, and prolific author in Zurich, who published a Hebrew grammar and a revised Latin version of the Qur'an.

Martin Bucer (1491–1551): leading reformer in Strasbourg and irenic theologian who died in England.

John Bugenhagen (1485–1558): former monk from Pomerania, who became pastor and professor in Wittenberg and the organizer of Lutheran churches in north Germany.

Henry Bullinger (1504–75): *Zwingli*'s long-term successor as head of the Reformed Zurich church.

Thomas Cajetan (1469–1534): born James de Vio in Italy, Cajetan became a learned theologian, general of the Dominican order, a distinguished cardinal, and papal legate; in 1518, he failed to obtain Luther's submission at Augsburg, and later he was sent to Hungary to encourage Christians against the Turks.

John Calvin (1509–64): chief reformer in Geneva beginning in 1541.

Wolfgang Capito (1478–1541): Humanist scholar, cathedral preacher in Basel and Mainz, reformer and colleague of *Bucer* in Strasbourg; in theology, Capito was closer to *Zwingli* than Luther, but he met the reformer on several occasions.

chapter of clergy: an endowed community of priests who are not monks, for example the All Saints' chapter in Wittenberg, usually connected to a cathedral or prominent church.

Charles V (1500–58): king of Spain, elected emperor of the *Holy Roman Empire* in 1519, before whom Luther appeared at the Diet of Worms in 1521.

confessions: statements of belief and practice adopted by Protestant churches during and after the Reformation to distinguish them from Roman Catholicism and from one another.

John Eck (1486–1543): skilled Catholic priest and theologian who debated Luther at Leipzig, opposed the Augsburg Confession, and participated in religious dialogues with Protestants.

electors: after 1356, four rulers of secular territories, of which Saxony was one, and three rulers of church lands, who were charged with electing the emperor of the *Holy Roman Empire*.

Friedrich Engels (1820–95): German political theorist, co-author with Marx of the *Communist Manifesto*, and author of *The German Peasants' War* (1894).

Erasmus of Rotterdam (c. 1469–1536): eminent Dutch Humanist who remained loyal to Rome and defended free choice of the human will against Luther.

estates: free cities (like Nuremberg), church lands (like Mainz), and secular territories (like Hesse and Saxony) that were entitled to send delegates and rulers to the diets of the *Holy Roman Empire*.

evangelical (from *evangelisch*): German term for the earliest supporters of reform and used later with church names like Lutheran and Reformed; equivalent to Protestant and not to be confused with modern non-denominational evangelicals.

Frederick the Wise (1463–1525): Frederick III, elector of Saxony, built a new castle and church in Wittenberg, enriched the All Saints' chapter, established the university, and protected Luther from the imperial ban.

Argula von Grumbach (c. 1490–1564): Bavarian noblewoman who wrote on behalf of the Reformation and visited Luther at the Coburg.

Johann Gottfried Herder (1744–1803): German philosopher, theologian, literary critic, friend of Goethe, and church superintendent in Weimar.

Karl Holl (1866–1926): professor of church history in Berlin; his Reformation anniversary lecture in 1917 on Luther's understanding of religion and his other essays initiated a renaissance of Luther studies.

Holy Roman Empire (962–1806): considered the medieval successor of the Roman Empire; by 1521, its dominion was larger than Germany and consisted of 383 separate *estates*.

Justus Jonas (1493–1555): professor of law and theology in Wittenberg, pastor, translator, and close friend of Luther who was present in Worms, at the reformer's wedding, and at his deathbed.

Andrew Karlstadt (1486–1541): Luther's colleague who initiated changes in Wittenberg but was forced out after Luther's return from the Wartburg.

Wenzel Linck (1483–1547): Luther's friend and *Augustinian* prior in Wittenberg, present at Augsburg (1518) and Leipzig (1519), briefly vicar-general of the strict Augustinians before becoming an evangelical preacher and reformer in Altenburg and Nuremberg.

Philip Melanchthon (1497–1560): layman from south Germany, co-reformer with Luther and his successor in Wittenberg, Humanist scholar, prolific author, religious negotiator, and leading theologian at Augsburg.

Thomas Müntzer (before 1490–1525): priest, student in Wittenberg, mystical theologian, severe critic of Luther, and prophet of the thousand-year reign of Christ; captured in the revolution of 1525 and executed.

Friedrich Nietzsche (1844–1900): son of a Lutheran pastor, influential German philosopher, and critic of his society's Christian moralism.

Philip of Hesse (1504–67): landgrave of Hesse and prominent Protestant leader converted by Melanchthon; he lost power after he committed bigamy and was defeated and imprisoned by Charles V in 1547.

Urbanus Rhegius (1489–1541): Humanist scholar, theologian, and Lutheran reformer both in Augsburg and in north-central Germany; he never saw Wittenberg but visited Luther at the Coburg in 1530.

Katharina Schütz Zell (1497–1562): author and reformer in Strasbourg.

George Spalatin (1484–1545): served as librarian, chaplain, and secretary to *Frederick the Wise*; intermediary between Luther and Frederick and the reformer's most frequent correspondent.

Johann von Staupitz (1460/69–1525): vicar-general of the observant *Augustinians*, theologian in Wittenberg who groomed Luther to succeed him, and spiritual adviser of the reformer.

Johann Walther (1496–1570): cantor and composer in Wittenberg and Torgau, friend of Luther, and editor of the first Lutheran hymnal (1524).

John Wesley (1703–91): Anglican clergyman, inspired by Moravian pietism, who founded the Methodist movement.

Ulrich Zwingli (1484–1531): main reformer in Zurich and Luther's primary opponent in the Lord's Supper controversy.

Index

Index